Dedication

This interactive workbook and textbook combination is dedicated first to the Holy Spirit, the true author, and an amazing guide!

Second, to Arthur Montgomery, who for the last twenty plus years has gone around the world preaching the gospel and sharing God's love with everyone and anyone who will hear it. I have never seen him turn someone down with a need for healing or deliverance. As a senior citizen, he still goes all over San Diego and really the world, just to see people set free. He has an incredible heart, and I have been super blessed to have him as a friend and a mentor in raising up an Army to carry out the marching orders of the King of Kings.

Third, it is dedicated to my parents, who homeschooled my five brothers and I, and spent long nights reading stories of the great men of God from history: Kenneth Hagin, Oral Roberts, Smith Wigglesworth etc., and filling our minds and our hearts with the stories of the Kingdom of Heaven. I also want to thank my amazing editors and contributors: Linda Staehr, Stan Donn and Matthew Wisan.

Lastly, it is dedicated to the incredible consistency of all the YouTube evangelists as well as all the Church Tsidkenu leaders and mentors who have gone out on the streets and to conferences day after day, healing, teaching and mentoring in how to move in the power of God. Without them, it's possible we would have continued in a generation without ever getting disciplined in how to move in God's power. To YouTube, specifically to Todd White, Pete Cabrera Jr., Tom Loud, Doug Collins, Torben Sondergaard, Tom Fischer, Shawn Hurley, and all the others I have missed.

Introduction

As a Church and an Academy, our goal is to empower Christians to walk in the full Mark 16 power of God, and in a strong relationship with the Holy Spirit and the Word. Throughout this book, we will be quoting the New King James translation.

The goal of this book is to provide a hands-on, practical approach to moving in the supernatural power of God, and to instruct in accelerating this power through a strong relationship with Holy Spirit. We have done many conferences and mission trips and seen thousands activated in the power of God. We want to activate and empower Christians everywhere to walk in the power of God that is already inside them. As the world tries to get darker, we will shine brighter!

The dinner bell for salvation rings in healings, deliverance, word of knowledge, word of wisdom, prophecy, baptizing in the Holy Spirit and Fire and all the supernatural. We will be presenting how to do all of these in this book so that you may bring glory to God. Remember in Mark 16:15, Jesus says to "go into all the world and preach the gospel and these signs will follow those who believe." He then lists five miracles that will prove to people that the gospel is real! *"And these signs will follow those who believe: In My name they will cast out demons; they will speak with new tongues; they will take up serpents; and if they drink anything deadly, it will by no means hurt them; they will lay hands on the sick, and they will recover."* (Mark 16:17-18) Jesus even said His generation would not have had sin if He didn't do the miracles of His father (John 15:24)! Performing miracles as you preach the gospel gives God the opportunity to confirm your words, with His power! And guys, it works very well! People say California and many states in America are "hard ground" spiritually, but we have seen hundreds and hundreds on the streets, in rehabs, in malls, on beaches in California and all over America give their lives to Jesus and get baptized in Holy Spirit and Fire. All of this because we believe in showing the power of God as we preach, everywhere we preach, people are getting healed, demons are getting cast out, and souls are being saved. Let's win our generation with the gospel and with the love and power of God!

We are going to jump right into this!

Three months ago, I was trying to go to sleep and all of a sudden, I felt the presence of God in my room. I felt my whole lower body turn numb and the Holy Spirit spoke to me and I saw a vision of an angel. The angel spoke to me and said, "You have been thinking about a revival in America the wrong way; it will come like before as well, but there is a new thing I am doing. I am calling you not to a revival but to raise up an army to declare war on the religious spirit that has taken over my people in America. Not a war on a people or on institutions or on churches, but against a spirit. Set my people free, and teach them to walk in the full power of the gospel."

The purpose of this workbook is to do just that. To empower Christians everywhere, with the hands-on knowledge of how to move in the supernatural, and thereby lead people to Jesus. To teach people how to practically fulfill the great commission described in Mark 16.

This workbook integrates theory and theology with application. As it says in James, faith without corresponding actions is dead. Too many times these days we are taught <u>what</u> to do, but are not first given <u>the ability to practice and to demonstrate it</u>.

If we look closely at Jesus's ministry and discipleship program, He would teach for hours, and heal and cast out demons. He would also subject His disciples to practice all of the time. For example, when He sent out the seventy on their first mission trip, they hadn't been with Him for very long, they came back rejoicing and talking about all the miracles they saw.

Our goal with this interactive workbook is to give you the resources and hands-on know-how to practice everything that God has downloaded inside you so we <u>can</u> fulfill the great commission in America and in the world!

Each Week explains how to operate in one or more of the gifts which we are commanded to move in, while fulfilling the great commission with a strong focus on developing our character and relationship with each other and with God.

For example, the first few weeks are focused on developing a strong character and relationship with God and His Holy Spirit, so we can get closer to Him and also move in the power of God. They are also focused on addressing typical issues that come up in our lives as we go from being a natural to a supernatural Christian.

In John 15:7, Jesus says, *"If you abide in Me, and My Words abide in you, you will ask what you desire, and it shall be done for you."* He makes it very clear, "if you abide in me you will bear fruit", as we spend time with God, get discipled, and go on the streets, we will see amazing fruit! As we take the lessons in the first few Weeks to heart, we will see a dramatic increase of relationship with God and power as we go out. As we abide, we bear fruit.

We expect that most readers will we be completely transformed by these teachings and lessons, and by the end of these sixteen weeks will walk more in power and authority than ever before in life. But your success is based on you.

The transformation will only come if you do and act on what we are teaching, and don't just read it. This book and the assignments are to motivate action, not just to become a thought process, or a point of debate. This workbook and school will train you into becoming the full, empowered men and women of God who you are, allowing the Holy Spirit to move through you, as unencumbered as He desires.

How to Read this book

Videos
In each of the Weeks, there are two or three YouTube videos to help with the audio/visual aspect of learning how to move in the supernatural.

As a side note, some of these videos are created by third-party ministers and are posted to the public domain. They are not a reflection of these ministers supporting this school or our ideals, and in no way represent a connection to them and this School or Church in any way.

Medical Advice
Anyone participating in this, or any Church Tsidkenu, affiliated event is participating at his or her own risk. Church Tsidkenu, or its affiliates, are not responsible for any injuries or complications that may occur. Church Tsidkenu and anyone associated with them or their events are not a medical doctor, attorney, psychiatrist, therapist or other licensed health professional. We do not diagnose, cure, heal, or treat disease, or give psychological treatment. We recommend that all participants continue to see their regular medical doctors and trained professional counselors and follow their advice as needed.

The founder is an ordained minister and our work is spiritually and biblically based. We believe these healings are based on God's Divine Power through His son Jesus. We do not make any promises, warranties or guarantees about the results of our healing work or the Divine guidance that we may receive and relay to people. Biblical Guidance and Healing sessions help many people, but like any modality, they may or may not work for all.

Style of Book

This is a combination of what would traditionally be called a textbook and a workbook. The goal of this book is to give a solid understanding of how to move in the supernatural power of God through personal anecdotes, stories and through the Word of God. It is also a workbook, that unlike many of its contemporaries, will guide you through step-by-step healing, deliverance and the other gifts with words, confessions, YouTube videos, and the best ACTIONS. Moving in God's power is actually incredibly simple; Jesus says "only believe." Because of this, I encourage you not to 'overthink it'; the goal of this book is not necessarily to build new theology, but to remove the lies and limitations that have been put forth by traditions of men, hindering our walk in the supernatural power of God.

Terms and Explanations

- Prayer - There are two types of prayer, and they reflect the greatest commandments. *Jesus said to him, "'You shall love the Lord your God with all your heart, with all your soul, and with all your mind.' This is the first and great commandment. And the second is like it: 'You shall love your neighbor as yourself.' On these two commandments hang all the Law and the Prophets."* (Matthew 22: 37-40) First is vertical prayer, which you carry out in your quiet time, and is more about an upward relationship with Him. The second is Horizontal Prayer, this is a prayer type where you pray for people around you.

- Praying in Tongues - This term describes entering in with the gift of tongues as talked about in the book of Acts.

- Outreach - This is a term used to describe our evangelistic pursuits typically outside of the contemporary church building.

How to Do Assignments and Homework

At the end of each of the Weeks, there will be assignments and homework. The class is structured all-inclusively, and is optimally effective when all the required reading, watching, and confessing is carried out.

We will be looking at different resources that you can use that will help speed up your coherency, expectancy, and results when praying for people. Regardless of what type of learner you are (visual, audio, hands-on, etc.), we have suitable resources so you can you to pick this up as quickly as possible. We have videos, books, confessions and hands-on options which will propel you into becoming proficient in walking in the graces of healing, deliverance and other gifts. If you are not in our online or in-person class, and are just reading this workbook, we really encourage you to get the required reading and go through it as you're reading along (if you have time, the suggested reading is very good too).

For the reading portion, I highly encourage you to get the five required books on the list, they are all chosen for very specific reasons, and will completely transform your lifestyle and expectancy.

For the watching portion, please take a few minutes and walk through the YouTube videos. We really want this to be a visual and audio experience as well as textual, so you learn as much as possible.

For the confessions, these are geared to get you speaking God's truth over your life daily, so you can experience His transformation optimally.

For the practice and application parts, please take them seriously as these are the most important parts of these classes; take time and do the assignments. I know sometimes it will be hard and may even be intimidating, but remember you are not on trial; it's God's power that goes into the nations. He will back up His Word.

Table of Contents

Week 1 - Our Relationship with Jesus: The Word of God

A. Teaching

This Week, we want to focus on developing your relationship with the Word of God. We need to first understand that the Word of God is not just a book inspired by God, but the Word is actually alive!

Relationship with the Word of God

In John 1:1 it says, *"In the beginning was the Word, and the Word was with God, and the Word was God."* John 1:14 says, *"And the Word became flesh and dwelt among us, and we beheld His glory, the glory as of the only begotten of the Father, full of grace and truth."* It's talking about Jesus. Mark 16:19 says, *"So then, after the Lord had spoken to them, He was received up into heaven, and sat down at the right hand of God."* Positionally, Jesus is at the right hand of the Father right now making intercession for the Saints. In John 16:7, when the disciples asked if they could go with Jesus, He said, *"Nevertheless I tell you the truth. It is to your advantage that I go away; for if I do not go away, the Helper will not come to you; but if I depart, I will send Him to you."* Therefore, since Jesus is not with us now, our primary relationship with Jesus is with the Word of God, both the Rhema (spoken, meditated, muttered) and the Logos (read Word of God). If we have a relationship with the Word of God, according to John 1, we have a relationship with Jesus.

I know of people who study the Word all the time, and some of them have had amazing actual visitations from Jesus; Kenneth E. Hagin was one of these. We have to remember it's His Word, and it's also actually Him.

Jesus represents the Logos and the Rhema - the written Word and the spoken Word. We need to stop thinking of a physical Jesus and start building a relationship with His Word. I am not saying that we don't have any relationship with Jesus without His Word, but I am saying for the contemporary believer, our main relationship with Jesus should be through His Word and through His Holy Spirit.

Why is a Relationship with the Father, Jesus, and Spirit So Important?

In Matthew 7:21-23, Jesus is talking to His disciples and saying that in the last days, many will come and say to Him, "*Lord, Lord, have we not prophesied in Your name, cast out demons in Your name, and done many wonders in Your name? And then I will declare to them, 'I never knew you; depart from Me, you who practice lawlessness!'*"

Some take this scripture out of context, and try to cast a dispersion on the supernatural, but the Word "knew" in the Greek is ginōskō and is talking about a deep intimacy with God - so close spiritually that the same word is used when two married people come together physically.

He is saying, depart from me, you who have worked miracles but have not had a deep relationship with me. Remember, the number one commandment of all time is to Love God and the second is to love people. Walking in miracles and healings is so important and is part of the second most important commandment in the whole Bible, that is that if you love your brother, you don't want him to stay in the same desperate position - you will heal him, deliver him, etc. But healing and deliverance do not <u>replace</u> the first and number one commandment, but you are fulfilling Mark 16 by healing, preaching, delivering and raising, thus obeying the second most important commandment.

Make sure you keep your relationship, through daily time in the Word and prayer, consecrated

Further Greek explanations:

- ☐ Ginōskō – to know properly, especially through personal experience (first-hand acquaintance).

- ☐ "Experientially know" is used for example in Luke 1:34, "And Mary [a virgin] said to the angel, "How will this be since I do not know (sexual intimacy) a man?" (Strongs 1097)

- ☐ The word anomía in Matthew 7:23 (*And then I will declare to them, 'I never knew you; depart from Me, you who practice lawlessness!'*) means lawlessness and literally means without the law; and so again the point is, performing miracles will not save you alone, you need to have a relationship and be obedient to God's Word. With all this in mind, one of Jesus's main commandments is to heal the sick, raise the dead, cast out demons and preach the gospel. anomía ("not" and nómos, "law") – properly, without law; lawlessness; the utter disregard for God's law (His written and living Word) (Strongs 458).

Enjoy your relationship with God daily, and now let's save the world with the POWER OF GOD.

Meditating or Speaking God's Word Over Our Lives Daily

In Joshua 1:8, it says to meditate on God's Word day and night and to not let it depart from our lips. Psalms 1:2 says to keep the Word of God in front of our eyes and to meditate on it, day and night. It's so important to always be in the Word of God. Remember John 15:7, *"If you abide in Me, and My Words abide in you, you will ask what you desire, and it shall be done for you."* Also, remember in Romans 10:17 how we get our faith, *"So then faith comes by hearing, and hearing by the Word of God."* As we study the Word, especially out loud - as we quote it, speak it over our lives, we will start to see a transformation. It's not enough just to read it, we need to speak the Word of God over our lives.

In Hebrew, 'word' means to mutter (hagah) or to speak God's Word over our lives (Strongs 1897). It is so important for us to learn to speak the Word of God over us. Remember, the Proverbs 18:21 says that *"life and death are in the power of the tongue."* James 3:6 talks about controlling the tongue. The world was created by God out of the Words of His mouth (Genesis 1:3). We can create our realities daily with the words out of our mouths. We need to be careful what we say or don't say, and learn to convert our language to God's truth.

Whether it is in declaring that a miracle will happen before we see it, or in speaking God's truth about our finances or life, we need to learn to speak His Words and His light over our lives regardless of what we see. Many times, things in our lives won't shift until we start to speak them out in our words. The spoken truth of God's Word will cancel the changing "facts" of life. We need to start speaking, and we will see the change in our lives and others that we desire to see!

Becoming One with the Word of God

There's a great paraphrase from one of Todd White's videos that talks about John 1. He says, "in the beginning, was the Word of God and the Word became flesh so that our flesh could become all word!" I believe that God wants to convert us to becoming one will and one heart with the Father by the continual renewing of the Word and through prayer.

Romans 12:2 says, *"And do not be conformed to this world, but be transformed by the renewing of your mind, that you may prove what is that good and acceptable and perfect will of God."*

James 1:21 says *"receive with meekness the implanted Word, which is able to save your souls."*

Proverbs 3:8 and 4:22 say, *"It will be health to your flesh, And strength to your bones."* and *"For they are life to those who find them, And health to all their flesh."*

God wants us to transform our carnal or natural minds until they match up with the true Word of God. We are called to be one with God in John 17:11b, *"Holy Father, keep through Your name those whom You have given Me, that they may be one as We are."* This is so important in our walk!

The Word Will Increase Your Power

When I am constantly abiding in the Word and I do outreach, honestly, healings and deliverances are so much easier. They just happen all around me. One of the tricks to walking in the fullness of healing that God wants is to STAY IN THE WORD.

I also like to stop and meditate for five to ten minutes on one verse where Jesus heals someone and as I go over that verse twenty to thirty times, my faith increases like crazy.

I have noticed in my life that as I am abiding in His Word, that miracles, healings, and deliverances just flow out so easily. If you want to see bigger miracles, then start meditating on the crazy healing scriptures, like dead raising and creative miracles. This will create an expectant heart for the big stuff. Remember in Romans 10:17 it says that *"faith comes by hearing and hearing by the Word of God!"* John 15:7 says, *"If you abide in Me, and My Words abide in you, you will ask what you desire, and it shall be done for you."*

The Power of Communion

Another huge point is on the power of communion. We need to take communion daily and have a fresh commitment to Jesus daily, Jesus teaches us to take up our cross daily (Luke 9:23). Many of the great men of God took communion each day, Smith Wigglesworth among these. There is a supernatural power that comes from this daily consecration and dedication that will increase in your life and in the power in which you walk. The Holy Spirit's power increases in your life based on your consecration and on your ability to be a set apart vessel (2 Timothy 2:21).

Communion is a faith act that is like a mini-rededication and a renewal of your relationship with Jesus, and your understanding of the price He paid. (It's also a chance to turn away from any sin that has tried to creep into your life.) *"This cup is the new covenant in My blood. Do this, as often as you drink it, in remembrance of Me."* (1 Corinthians 11:25). When we take communion, we are spiritually relying on God for our sustenance and acknowledging and remembering the covenant. As we drink the juice and eat the bread by faith, our hearts become aware again of our relationships with Jesus. This is one of the main reasons there is so much power in communion - because it's a rededication, a consecration to our first love, Jesus. Remember, the two biggest things that follow an increase in consecration are an <u>increase in depth</u> of relationship with Jesus and an <u>increase of power</u> in our daily lives! An increase of consecration, whether it's in more time in the Word, in Prayer, hitting the streets with the Good News or just a simple act of obedience, will always increase the Power of God on your lives!

B. Research, Activation, and Resources

Reading

> **Bible** - At least three chapters a day, Beginning in Matthew. Meditate on Psalms 1 and Joshua 1.
>
> **Textbook** - Week 2
>
> **Required Reading** - <u>The Believer's Authority</u>, Kenneth E. Hagin

Suggested Reading - <u>Atomic Power with God, Thru Fasting and Prayer</u>, Franklin Hall

Watching:

Church Tsidkenu - MUTE man TALKS in JESUS NAME!! HAHA!

https://www.youtube.com/watch?v=gqoeLWwKRQU&feature=youtu.be

Art Montgomery - JESUS APPEARS 2 TIMES DURING DELIVERANCE

https://www.youtube.com/watch?v=JoTQGbqoLPw&t=102s

Kenneth Hagin - God's Word is Food

https://www.youtube.com/watch?v=rKwSSlzWhrk

Bill Winston - The Law of Confession:

https://www.youtube.com/watch?v=Qr0VbJM9cEI

Speaking

1. **Commit to finding at least three areas of your life to start speaking God's truth over.**
2. Find an area of need (health, finances, fear).
3. Find a verse that has God's truth on the matter and make it first person.
4. Speak this verse over the area at least ten times a day as part of your quiet time.

Doing

Find an area in your life that you know God's Word but are not being obedient and choose some practical steps to help you obey. Ask the Holy Spirit for help if you need it. For example: When I first started as a Christian, I found that being kind to people who were mean to me wasn't natural for me, but God's Word is very clear about loving people. Because of this, I started choosing to walk in love towards people; it changed them and me.

Passing - Assignments are Due at the Beginning of the Following Class.

A. Teaching

It's very important that we understand the role of the Holy Spirit, and our need to have a strong relationship with Him. The current church treats the Holy Spirit as a mystical presence, a wind, a breeze, a soft feeling, goosebumps. Art Montgomery tells of God speaking to him and saying, "The church treats me like an angel, and I'm God!" The problem with this is we limit Him to a whimsical, mystical feeling. In reality, the Holy Spirit has a personality. The Greek word for Spirit is Pneuma (Strong's G4151 - pneuma), meaning breath or wind of God. The Holy Spirit is the presence or essence of God. He needs to be honored, spoken to and respected.

We Don't Need to be Afraid

Something else important is that the Holy Spirit is here to help us; we do not need to be afraid of the Holy Spirit, but we need to run towards, not away from Him. Jesus said, *"If a son asks for bread from any father among you, will he give him a stone? Or if he asks for a fish, will he give him a serpent instead of a fish? Or if he asks for an egg, will he offer him a scorpion? If you then, being evil, know how to give good gifts to your children, how much more will your heavenly Father give the Holy Spirit to those who ask Him!"* (Luke 11:11-13)

In other words, the Holy Spirit is a Great Gift! There is nothing you need to fear. Remember, He won't give you a deceptive spirit, kundalini, witchcraft, etc. "a serpent, or a scorpion." Jesus is normally referring to the demonic when talking about snakes and scorpions (Luke 10:19). It's time to start talking to the Holy Spirit and treating Him like a person. He is the presence of God; the church treats him like a mystical presence or an angel, but he is the Spirit of the living God. Jesus instructs us to rely on Him for comfort, instruction, direction, insight, and encouragement. John 14:26 says, *"But the Helper, the Holy Spirit, whom the Father will send in My name, He will teach you all things, and bring to your remembrance all things that I said to you."* We need to realize that He is the only person of the Godhead we have here on Earth and inside of us. If we are afraid of Him or of talking to Him, He can't help us.

We need to understand who the Holy Spirit is. The Holy Spirit is not a mystical presence, He is not goosebumps, He is not a feeling or a breeze. The Holy Spirit is an actual Person, and He is the third part of the Trinity. The easiest way of saying it would be, that the Holy Spirit is the Personality and the Person of the Presence of God.

What is He for?

This is a great question, and one that most of the church does not seem to understand. Biblically, the Holy Spirit's role is a coach, teacher, and comforter throughout life; He is more personal and the only part of the Trinity who is actually with us on earth. To put it clearly, the role of the Holy Spirit is to be our teacher, our guide, our comforter, and our helper, to lead us into all truth and take the place of having the physical Jesus with us every day.

Jesus says, *"it is better that I go, so He will come"* (John 16:7).

We understand in John 14:18 when Jesus said, *"I will not leave you orphans; I will come to you,"* that where Jesus is going, we can't come yet. Jesus said in John 13:36 when, *"Simon Peter said to Him, "Lord, where are You going?" Jesus answered him, "Where I am going you cannot follow Me now, but you shall follow Me afterward."* We see in 1 John 2:27, with the Holy Spirit, we have no need that any man teaches us anything because the Holy Spirit will lead us into all truth.

The role of the Holy Spirit is one of the most overlooked in the contemporary church. In a time when megachurches are on the rise, and we listen to podcasts and pastors all the time, it is very easy to neglect the role of the Holy Spirit. The Bible also says that the Holy Spirit will bring to remembrance the Words I've spoken to you (John 14:26). In other words, He wants to teach us daily, and remind us in a practical and personal way what Jesus is saying.

The main difference between a pastor's advice, or reading the Bible, is the Holy Spirit will give revelation and wisdom that is specific to you since he lives inside of you; He knows you better than any human ever could. God says *"there is a friend who sticks closer than a brother"* (Proverbs 18:24). We see that the presence of God living inside of us as a more intimate relationship with us than anyone, and because of this can provide us with more insight than any other person. If we look at the church in Acts, they are led all around the world by the Holy Spirit. Many times, if they did not have that leading, they would be lost, or be in danger.

One of the main roles of the Holy Spirit is to be our guide. Many times, and in charismatic circles, we live according to signs that we see, or words that we get from prophecy. Now both of these are biblical in the right context. But in the wrong context, they can replace the still small voice. We understand that publicly we are supposed to be led by the Holy Spirit. He is our teacher and our guide. Words of prophecy and signs are supposed to be a confirmation for what we know already from the Holy Spirit because he is our guide.

The modern church has completely minimized the power of and the ROLE of the Holy Spirit, and because of this, there is much deception and confusion in the church. The Bible says that the Holy Spirit will lead us into all truth. If we are not putting a focus on the One who wants to lead us into all truth, we are most likely walking in error or confusion.

Talk to Him Specifically

It's very important for us to put an emphasis on the Holy Spirit because Jesus said to do it. Some people argue, "Well, if I have a relationship with Jesus isn't that the same thing?" This is not correct since each part of the Trinity is a specific Being, and has a different relationship with us; we benefit from each of these relationships.

Yes, they are three in one, but they are three specific entities, with three specific characteristics. Otherwise, Jesus would not have made the distinction of Him leaving, and the

Holy Spirit staying. Our focus on the Holy Spirit is a choice of obedience because Jesus said to do it. One of the biggest errors in the contemporary church is over-looking the role of the Holy Spirit in the believer's everyday life.

We need to learn to communicate and have communion with the Holy Spirit daily. He is not some weird mystical presence, but He is the presence of God in the same way that Jesus is the Word of God. We need to have a relationship with both Persons, and of course a relationship with God the Father.

Holy Spirit Acceleration

One of the goals of the Holy Spirit is an acceleration of the supernatural. We see all the time, hundreds and hundreds of people healed when we honor the Holy Spirit. We need to include Him in a big way in deliverance, healing, street ministry, etc. Since Jesus said to put your focus on the Holy Spirit, we encourage our people to overdo it with the Holy Spirit, since the contemporary churches underdo it. Obviously, we are not suggesting to turn from a strong foundation in the Word of God, but we need to be not 50%, but 100% towards the Word of God and the Holy Spirit!

If we have too much Word without the Holy Spirit, it's easy to get dry. 2 Corinthians 3:6 says, *"who also made us sufficient as ministers of the new covenant, not of the letter but of the Spirit; for the letter kills, but the Spirit gives life."* But if we have too much Holy Spirit without a good foundation in the Word, it's easy to get flaky. We need to learn how to be balanced followers of Jesus.

Honestly, we need to invite the Holy Spirit into the supernatural when we're walking in it. When I'm doing deliverance I often say, 'Holy Spirit what's really going on? Show me.' When I'm praying for healing and I'm not seeing it, I often say, 'Holy Spirit show me what really needs to happen.' When I'm in the middle of a sozo (see Week 10) and I'm not sure how to help the person, I often pray, 'Holy Spirit show me how to help them and what key they need to unlock the hurt.' And when I am on a mission trip and I'm not sure where to turn, or there's danger, I always pray and He always shows up. We really need to learn how to allow the Holy Spirit to accelerate the supernatural gifts!

Jesus says *"if I through the finger of God"* in one translation, or in another book *"if I through the Holy Spirit drive out demons."* (Luke 11:20, Matthew 12:28) We understand that the Holy Spirit is the finger of God; we understand that all the gifts are through the Holy Spirit.

If we invite Him into outreach, into deliverance, and to healings, we will see a greater manifestation of God's Love and Power greater than ever before. Our ministry started taking off when we started asking the Holy Spirit not to just show up, but to take over, and really meant it! Revival will come out of an honoring of the personhood of the Presence of God.

A Quick Word About Church and the Holy Spirit

I will not say much on this point, but the truth is the Holy Spirit is micromanaged in many churches, and therefore the freedom to individuals that God wants to bring gets very quenched, along with the deliverance and the healing.

There's so much liberty that God wants to bring to the contemporary church if we could just learn to let go of the reins and let Him show up. Revival comes by letting God move. Many times we say, "Holy Spirit come; Holy Spirit show up", but when He does, we don't like to lose our control, and so nothing changes.

To see a revival in our churches and reformation as a whole, we have to release control to the One whose house it really is; keep order, but release control. Jesus did not even call it His house, He said it's my Father's house (Matthew 21:12-13). In the house of God, should not His Presence be allowed to move throughout the services?

Hearing God's Voice

The role of the Holy Spirit is so important in guiding and teaching us and letting us hear God's voice. One of the coolest side effects of doing street outreach, and ministry to others, is we start to learn to hear and discern God's voice through His Holy Spirit out of necessity.

I would encourage you if you ever meet an obstacle to instantly say, "Holy Spirit show me what's really going on here." I would encourage you before you start a deliverance or word of knowledge, learn to partner with the Holy Spirit, and ask Him to show you what's really going on. This has been one of the biggest transformations in my life and in our student's lives.

I would also encourage you to shift your thinking of the Holy Spirit from an energy, a metaphysical presence, goosebumps, a warm fuzzy feeling, to the actual presence, personality and personhood of the living God. We are invited to have an intimate deep relationship with Him in the same way a child has a relationship with a loving, supportive parent and teacher. He wants to be a huge part of your life and bring revelation to every area. Just acknowledge Him and include Him, and most importantly talk to Him. Without Him, our lives are full of confusion and frustration.

Prayer

One of the most effective ways to get and stay filled with the Holy Spirit is through praying in other tongues for a prolonged time. *"So He Himself often withdrew into the wilderness and prayed."* (Luke 5:16) *"Now it came to pass in those days that He went out to the mountain to pray, and continued all night in prayer to God."* (Luke 6:12).

Jesus taught His disciples how to pray and how to pray a lot. He said in one verse, "can't you even spend one hour with Me?" Prayer has been a powerful weapon of transformation for myself (obviously the Word as well) and the key to the transformation of every place and location I enter. In the Bible, there were specific hours of prayer; most other religions have set prayer times. Prayer is a spiritual discipline that we need to develop in our personal lives if we really want to see the personal and national transformation that we say we do.

My Story

When I first got interested in God, I had a massive hunger, but I wanted to know it was real. I remember at the age of 7, seeing people get touched in church and out of frustration praying "God teach me how to love you!" Nine years later I was 16 and very frustrated, I would be good one week and bad another, even then I knew this wasn't real transformation or real righteousness. I remember, that weekend one of my brothers was having orthodontic surgery so I had more time on my hands. I read The Cross and the Switchblade by David Wilkerson. There he talks about making a deal with God and saying that as an experiment, he was going to exchange his 2 hours of watching television every night for two hours of prayer. After he did that a few months, God called him to use this prayer time to transform his life. He used him to start Teen Challenge, which since then has been responsible for setting free millions of young men and women from gangs, drugs and horrible lifestyles. After I read this, I made a deal as well. I said God, "I have tried to change myself and I know I can't. If you're real I am going to put it to the test. I will give you one year of my life, I am going to pray every night for 2 hours, but here's the deal. I am done trying to change myself, so during this time I am going to stop trying. If I change, I will know You are real, and will give You my life, if not, I have the next 80 years to do whatever I want." The way I saw it, one year of consecration was a small price to pay. If God was real, I would know it and if not, I would still have the rest of my life to do whatever I wanted. Let me tell you, in that 3 months everything changed! I went from introvert to extrovert, from no love for others to massive love and compassion, from sadness to joy, EVERYTHING CHANGED! Then I said, "God you can have my life, it's all yours"! That was 15 years ago, since then I have prayed on average of 1-2 hours every day. Out of my prayer closet, I had many things I am praying for materialize - my businesses, my wife, the movements and churches God has had me plant. Because of this, John 15:5 has become so so alive to me, "I am the vine, you are the branches. He who abides in Me, and I in him, bears much fruit; for without Me you can do nothing." Guys, this is so so true, if you will seek God in private, He will reward you openly, and use you to CHANGE THE WORLD! Consecration is the key to the revival we are looking for, and prayer is the one of the most important parts of consecration!

Duration of Time

We see that prayer was an integral part of Jewish culture in the times of Jesus, much more than it is now. I would venture to say, one of the big problems in the church is a lack of consecration outside of the church during the week in daily alone time in the secret place, time spent in prayer and in the Word.

Most theologians say that during biblical days, there were three different times of prayer throughout the day, typically 9 am, 12 pm and 3 pm. Everyone would stop what they were doing and just pray; it was an integral part of the Jews and the disciples' culture of consecration (Daniel 6:10, Psalms 55:17, Acts 2:15, Acts 10:9). This was a culture of prayer, of consecration, and of the secrets of relationship depth with the Holy Spirit, and for the ever-increasing power flowing through them. In today's society and culture as a whole, studies show there is less consecration in prayer time. Some studies show the average Christian prays about 1 minute a day. We have busy lifestyles and it's easy to make excuses. But I promise you that it's worth it. Anytime you give to prayer, God will reward you, multiply your time and give it back to you!

How long should we pray? In Matthew 26:40, Jesus is teaching the disciples how to pray, because it is so key to their lives and they keep falling asleep. He finally says, "could ye not watch with Me one hour? Watch and pray, that ye enter not into temptation." Because of this, I would say a good standard time for prayer would be one hour a day. If you need to, you can work up to this as well, say start with twenty minutes, then forty minutes then sixty minutes. That being said, when we teach prayer in our schools and our churches, we encourage people to ask the Holy Spirit what time duration and time of day is good for them and their lives specifically.

Perseverance

It's important to know that the first couple of weeks to develop these new habits will be the hardest, since your mind will be fighting you. You will have thoughts of hunger, distraction, social media, everything, and impulses to do random stuff immediately. But if you push through these and stay consistent, a flow will open up and you will feel God's Presence like never before.

I started praying when I was sixteen for two hours each day and it changed my life. The first week was tough, but I pushed through it; fast-forward fifteen years later and I have had business come out of my prayer closet, churches, movements, my wife, really everything I value in my life has been out of just praying and being in relationship with God, and then acting on the direction I get. For years now, my prayer life is my most favorite thing to do each day! My secret though, is to return to prayer each day, especially if I have a hard day, or if I feel I missed God's voice. Choose to make prayer a part of your daily life for the rest of your life. It's not one powerful prayer necessarily, but the perseverance in prayer time daily that gets you to see and achieve your promises!

No Condemnation

Don't make it a religious thing or feel condemned if you miss a day here or there; every day is a little different in life. Also, don't feel you need to prayer for that exact time. Find your time that is best for you; it might be less, it might be more, just ask the Holy Spirit about what specifics work for you and your life. Although you should give your prayer life a pretty high priority compared to other things in your life, don't consistently skip work or classes or important things to pray more, find a good balance. The most important is to hear from Him. My goal is to pray and read for two hours each day, and I normally can do it, but not always. Your salvation and righteousness is through Jesus' sacrifice, and your faith is in this alone. Praying or reading more doesn't save you or change your standing of being an heir, but it's one of the better ways to grow in relationship with God and in His power. Like He said, when you pray in secret, He will reward you openly, and He definitely does. Remember that one demon, who didn't come out? The disciples asked why, and Jesus said that the disciples needed to be in more prayer and fasting (Matthew 17:21).

Pray Often

Jesus would often go to the lonely places and pray! We see the angels appearing to Peter while he is on the rooftop in deep prayer. I encourage people to pray for at least one hour one time a day or split it up into different prayer times.

Prayer is one of the most important parts of walking in the power of God and staying in the Spirit. You will be able to walk longer and with much more consistency if you have a strong prayer life. There will also be doors that you are not able to go through effectively for missions and evangelism if you are not in a strong place of prayer. If you have an apostolic calling, you will need a strong prayer life to provide a covering for the churches and ministries where God has you planted (John 17).

A Servant is Not Greater

Jesus walked in the power of the Holy Spirit without measure. He had full power and full anointing, but He still found the need to go and pray often. How much more do we need to be in a lifestyle of prayer? Someone says, 'Well this is all great, but I'm not Jesus.' Jesus said, *"A servant is not greater than his master"* (John 15:20). If Jesus had all power and was the full son of God in full communion with the Father and needed to pray a lot, how much more do we?

Pray in Tongues

Paul says, *"I thank God I speak [pray] more in tongues than you all..."* (1 Corinthians 14:18). In Romans 8:26 says, *"Likewise the Spirit also helps in our weaknesses. For we do not know what we should pray for as we ought, but the Spirit Himself makes intercession for us with groanings which cannot be uttered."* Here it talks about praying out mysteries with groanings that don't have natural words attached to them, and making intercession for our weaknesses. He is talking about prayer. Ephesians 6:11 says, *"Put on the whole armor of God, that you may be able to stand against the wiles of the devil."* In the last instruction for warfare and putting on the armor, Paul talks about praying and watching in the Spirit.

Prayer is one of your main tools to experience relationship and transformation for yourself outside of your weekly services; to pray out your future and stay walking in the Spirit.

Some Helpful Tips on How to Pray Practically

Here are some steps that took me fifteen years to learn, that will really, really help you grow in your prayer life.

1. Find a quiet spot, preferably a closet or room where you can be by yourself, a car, or a safe, deserted nature place works too. Matthew 6:6 says, *"But you, when you pray, go into your room, and when you have shut your door, pray to your Father who is in the secret place; and your Father who sees in secret will reward you openly."* So first we need to get alone, find a safe spot, but the more alone the better.

2. Put your phone on silent and in the other room. Jesus says very clearly about prayer that *"the spirit is willing, but the flesh is weak"* (Matthew 26:41). Putting the phone in the other room helps your weak flesh not get distracted.

3. Find a digital timer or kitchen timer and set a timer for yourself with the time you want to pray. You can forget about time and just focus on God.

4. Put on worship music, this helps a lot with your focus and sets an atmosphere of holiness and prayer to help with the focus.

5. Three stances for prayer (these are natural tips that just help):

   ☐ Walk and pray. The disciples kept falling asleep and this helps with that A LOT (Matthew 26:40).

   ☐ If you can force yourself to not sleep, covering your eyes with something helps so much and creates incredible intimacy with God. In the Jewish tradition, they would cover their head with a prayer shawl to remove distractions.

   ☐ If your mind is confused or feels oppressed, put your own hands on your head and pray, pray, pray; you have power in your hands and this will clear your mind up.

6.   Right before you start, do these two things – repent/turn away in your heart from anything wrong you have done knowingly or unknowingly, and cast all your cares and frustrations on God, so you don't have a lot of thoughts bugging you when you start. Philippians 4:6-7 says, *"Be anxious for nothing, but in everything by prayer and supplication, with thanksgiving, let your requests be made known to God; and the peace of God, which surpasses all understanding, will guard your hearts and minds through Christ Jesus."*

7.   Lastly, I have found, it's always best to read and meditate on the Word for a bit before you pray, because then your mind is renewed and it's easier to get into your prayer time with boldness and anticipation.

Fasting

We don't have a significant time in this book to really cover fasting in its fullness. But I want to throw a couple things out there. First, most biblical fasts, including all the Daniel actual FASTS were purely water fasts (Daniel 10). In fact, the word in Greek means literally to be without food (Strongs 3521). Daniel had a least one time where he abstained from some foods and did eat others, but he does not refer to these as fasts (Daniel 1).

Now that being said, if needed, you can do more of a liquid diet fast. But biblically, and what I have found to be the most effective, is to go on a pure water fast (please consult medical professionals as needed). This understanding of the water fast is very important. I think many times we misunderstand what fasting is for, at least in the context of fasting and prayer. <u>Fasting is a focal lens for persevering prayer!</u> Jesus said: *"Watch and pray, lest you enter into temptation. The spirit indeed is willing, but the flesh is weak."* (Matthew 26:41).

Fasting shuts down your weak flesh and natural body, so your willing spirit-man can persevere in prayer!

B. Research, Activation, and Resources

Reading

      Bible - At least three Chapters a day, Beginning in Matthew. Meditate on John 15 and Acts 2.

      Textbook – Read the next Week.

Required Reading - <u>Good Morning Holy Spirit</u>, Benny Hinn

Suggested (Very Good) Reading - <u>Cross and the Switchblade</u>, David Wilkerson

Watching:

Art Montgomery - HOW TO STIR YOURSELF UP WITH TONGUES AND THE HOLY SPIRIT

https://www.youtube.com/watch?v=NdYEKzho-7Q

Church Tsidkenu - Deaf & Mostly Mute Guy Gets Healed

https://www.youtube.com/watch?v=7BbSzpttczE

Art Montgomery - 25 MUSLIMS GET CONVERTED BY THE POWER

https://www.youtube.com/watch?v=jAPFv83zj9k&t=311s

Speaking

Commit to saying ten times a day "I have the Holy Spirit and He is a Person and a Good Gift. I seek Him for Counsel and Comfort."

Doing

1. Commit to talking to the Holy Spirit each day. Invite Him into each situation and ask for wisdom from Him.

2. Practice Asking Him questions about little or big things in your life.

3. Find an area of your life you need revelation in.

4. Say, "Holy Spirit show me what to do, say or be in this area."

5. Wait on Him and listen for His voice.

6. Spend a significant amount of time (twenty to sixty minutes a day) in prayer this week.

Passing

Assignments are due at the Beginning of the Following Class.

☐ Have you been able to identify and write down two main scriptures that talk about the importance of being God's Word?

Scripture 1_____

Scripture 2_____

☐ Have you read Week 2 in your workbook?

☐ Did you finish reading the Believer's Authority?

☐ Did you speak at least one truth of God's Word over your life at least ten time per day?

Week 3 - Relationship with the Father and His Other Kids

A. Teaching: The personality of the Father

Jesus always referred to God as the Father. He even starts His iconic prayer with "our Father", not My Father, but "our Father" (Matthew 6:9-13). We need to understand that God is a good Father. Jesus explains that God is not just a good Father, but a much better Father than any of us (Matthew 7:11). We see in the parable of the prodigal son, the incredible love of the Father, even when we are in the midst of horrible situations and sin (Luke 15:11-32). We need to understand that a huge part of Christianity as reinstating our perception and relationship with our true and loving Father.

To help us understand the Father's character, here are some Names of God, and the places in His Word where they appear:

> ELOHIM, the plural of One God; see Genesis 1: 1 & 2: 3
>
> ADONAI, Jehovah is Lord of Lightening, has risen, is exalted, of justice; see Genesis 15: 1-21
>
> EL ROI, God Who sees; see Genesis 16
>
> JEHOVAH JIREH, The Lord provides; see Genesis 22

EL SHADDAI, The Almighty God; see Genesis 28

YAWEH/JEHOVAH, The Great I AM; see Exodus 3

JEHOVAH ROPHE, The Lord Heals; see Exodus 15

JEHOVAH NISSI, The Lord my Banner; see Exodus 17

JEHOVAH MEKADESH, The Lord Who sanctifies; see Leviticus 20: 8-27

JEHOVAH SHALOM, The Lord is Peace; see Judges 6: 11-35

JEHOVAH SABAOTH, The Lord of Hosts; see 1 Samuel 1

JEHOVAH TSIDKENU, The Lord our Righteousness; see Jeremiah 23: 1-8

I would encourage people to start thinking of God more as their Father than even their natural dad. All our natural parents, though some may be great, are just people and cannot be there perfectly for us, so they fail us in one way or another. God is our spiritual Father, and this transcends any natural heritage we have. The more we think of God as our Father, the more we also accept His lineage and love.

The Lie about Who God is

There is a huge lie about God's love and who He is. God has incredible love for all of His children. We see this in Jesus' story about the prodigal son, that while the son was messing around and sinning, the Father was just waiting for him to come back. When the son finally came back, it was the son's own perspective that was getting in the way of His understanding of who His father really thought he was. But His father was running towards him with open arms, a robe of royalty, full of incredible, love and restoration.

Many times, our perspective gets in the way of how God really sees us. We need to open our eyes and open our hearts to the truth that God loves us so much. We will then be able to receive His love.

In Luke 15:19 the son says, *"I am no longer worthy to be called your son. Make me like one of your hired servants."* But we see as soon as he starts to head back, His father runs to him with open arms. This is how God views this, but imagine if the son let the lie get in the way of His perspective of himself and never came back to his father. We need to understand that God loves us so much. Never run away, but always run towards it Him regardless of where we have been or what we have done.

Abiding versus Working

We need to understand that God loves us and wants to transform us just through a relationship with Him.

Something that will change our lives is John 15, and understanding the concept behind it. In John 15, it says if we abide in Him, then we will bear fruit. We need to understand that much of our spiritual fruit of character and miracles will come as a byproduct of our relationship (John 15:5). This is why the top commandment in the Bible is *"Love the Lord your God with all your heart soul and mind and the second is love your neighbor as yourself."* (Luke 10:27). This is a perfect example of Mary and Martha. In the story, Martha is working for God, and Mary is just sitting with Jesus. Jesus says that Mary has chosen the better part (Luke 10:42). We need to understand that first, we have a relationship with God because He loves us, then we can do things for God. But our relationship with God cannot only depend on what we do for God. That is a dysfunctional and abusive relationship.

The Difference

This is also the difference between Jesus and the Pharisees. The Pharisees thought what they did justified them; Jesus knew that who He was more important. We need to rest in the fact that we are sons and daughters of God and enjoy pursuing a deep relationship with Him. Out of that relationship will come the desire to change and also the fruit of the Spirit, real fruit. The Bible says that if you abide, you bear fruit. Just by spending time with God, you will see the transformation that you desire.

For me, I started off as someone who kept trying to change himself and I saw zero consistent transformation; one week I was good, one week I was bad, but no real change. I said, 'God if you're real, I want to be a new creation like your Word promises; change me, make me, mold me! If not, then I'll just keep living life how I want to.' (2 Corinthians 5:17). I gave him a year of my life as a trial, and promised that if I change, I will know You are real; if I don't, I'll just keep doing what I know to do. I spent one to two hours in prayer and the Word every day, but here is the trick, I was not going to try and change myself any longer, it would just have to happen. I stopped trying to change myself and just started spending time in the Presence and Word of God. Three months into it I had changed so much that I knew that His Word is true. I gave Him my life! Since then, it's been fifteen years and I have had some of the best, most amazing times, and seen some of the coolest things I could've ever imagined. Just because of abiding with God. God is real and is a transformational being. If you spend time with Him and decide to do His commandments and trust Him to make you perfect in it, He will. We need to also understand that. It is very important for us for longevity, and is the truth to bearing much fruit.

The truth is that transformation comes out of a deep relationship with God, and takes the practical look of a daily relationship with Him through the Word and prayer. The more you do in the secret place as Jesus promises, the more He will reward you openly. And this has been so true in my life!

Remember God wants us to be with Him first, and then doing comes naturally. I've never seen an apple tree try and force apples out, it just sits calmly in the root system, and the fruit comes naturally. This is the same thing with us, if we spend time with the Father, the Holy Spirit and the Word of God on a daily basis; the fruit will just flow and we will be more worried about the abundance of fruit, than trying to force ourselves to produce it.

This has changed my life and will change yours! The church needs to spend more time in the closet with the Word and prayer, and it will then look completely different.

Second Commandment: Love People

The only true way to love people, and bear the fruit that is talked about in Galatians, is by abiding in the root system as it talks about in John 15. We need to abide so we can bear. But the most important fruit is love. It's important for us to judge the character of our lives based on our love walk.

In Corinthians, there's a whole chapter dedicated to love and it's right in between Corinthians 12 and Corinthians 14. In Corinthians 12, it talks about the different callings, gifts, and operations of the Holy Spirit. In Corinthians 14, it talks about the Holy Spirit leading service, praying in tongues and prophecy. In the middle of these two chapters is a huge chapter on LOVE. We must understand that there are two types of fruit in the Kingdom of Heaven. First is the fruit of character, and according to the Bible, this is summarized in loving our neighbor ~~by~~ as ourselves. That is our love walk. The second is the 'fruit of doing' or power, and this would be moving in the supernatural, saving the lost etc.; but the motive for all these miracles is still love and obedience. Both types of fruit are so important.

We can get in big trouble with God if we only display the fruit of power, and not the fruit of character. I would encourage everyone to ask the Holy Spirit to teach you how to love more and spend some time meditating on Corinthians 13 and all the verses in the Bible about loving your neighbor. It is the most important commandment outside loving God and should not be taken lightly.

As you spend time in the Word and in prayer, your love will start to change, but we need to choose in your heart to go with that change: to put others before you, to love unconditionally, and to lay your life down. Remember Jesus said, *"He who finds his life will lose it, and he who loses his life for My sake will find it."* (Matthew 10:39). *"Greater love has no one than this, than to lay down one's life for his friends."* (John 15:13)!

Never do anything that compromises your love walk towards your brothers and sisters. Love is not always positive encouragement, sometimes it's speaking the truth in love to someone when it's difficult for them to hear.

B. Research, Activation, and Resources

Reading:

    Bible - At least three chapters a day, beginning in Matthew. Meditate on John Luke 15:11-32.

    Textbook – Read the next Week

Watching:

    Bill Johnson - Jesus Came to Reveal the Father
    https://www.youtube.com/watch?v=3P5NEmJt9wE

    Art Montgomery - DRUG DEALER GET SLAIN BY SAYING
    https://www.youtube.com/watch?v=5e10kywdPCQ

Speaking

Commit to saying ten times a day "God is my real Father and He is a good Father. I decide to stop thinking of my earthly parents as my real parents and accept God as my real Father! All His DNA is mine with no mistakes, addictions or hurt. I have a huge inheritance." Psalms 27:10 says, *"When my father and my mother forsake me, then the Lord will take care of me."*

Doing

1. Decide in your heart to shift your perspective of God to one of a loving, Good Father.

2. Change how you think of your natural father

3. Decide to think of God as your Father and your natural father as your dad.

4. Start researching scriptures about God as a good Father.

5. Ask the Holy Spirit to Show you how God thinks of you.

Passing

Assignments are due at the beginning of the following class.

☐ Have you practiced this week asking the Holy Spirit questions about little or big things in your life?

☐ What did you hear from Him, what was the outcome?

_____

_____

_____

_____

_____

_____

_____

☐ Did you spend a significant amount of time (twenty to sixty minutes a day) in prayer daily?

☐ Have you read the next Week in your workbook?

☐ Did you finish reading the Good Morning Holy Spirit?

Week 4 - What is Your Identity?

A. Teaching

It's important for us to establish our identity. We have spent our whole life with people telling us what we are, how to think, what we need, want to look like. The problem with that is we can spend our whole life striving for something that isn't what God has for us today. The cool thing is that God said, "it was good" after He made everything; He said we were good soon as we were created (Genesis 1:31). We have to understand that we were perfect from day one; it says in Psalms 139:13 that God *"knit us together in our mother's womb."* Jesus says that children's angels are always before the Father's face (Matthew 18:10). We need to understand how perfect we are from day one, regardless of anything that we might think as imperfection.

Who does the Bible actually say we are?

It says that we are kings and priests; we are not just sons of God, we are sons of the living God Who created Heaven and Earth (Revelation 1:6). As sons of God, we are literally kings of the Earth. God told Adam to have dominion over the earth and over all of creation (Genesis 1:26-28). We were made to have dominion; another cool thought about this is the word dominion means to reign as a king. God intended for us to be kings of the Earth. After the fall of Adam, and then the death and resurrection of Jesus, this dominion was won back for us and restored through the name of Jesus and our identity as sons of God. Our identity before God is as a son of God, and therefore a king on the Earth. Philippians 2:3 says to esteem one another as higher than ourselves. Jesus said, *"he who would be greatest in the kingdom of God must become a servant of all"* (Mark 9:35).

So, our positional identity among our brothers and sisters in Christ is a servant's heart; we are called to be leaders. One of the strongest places we lead is from the front by doing, but also from the back by serving others. Jesus more often than not, would first lead by demonstrating the right way to live life and move in God, but He would always come back to serving the disciples.

Another Big Part of Identity is Confidence

Confidence is a huge thing; many times, the world misunderstands confidence as arrogance. There is nothing wrong with a healthy dose of confidence, and in fact, it is very difficult to lead ourselves or other people, or lead our family without it at some level. We just need to understand the origin of our confidence is in God. The difference between pride and confidence is, pride compares yourself to other people or the other beings, and always says you're better than anything or anyone. Confidence is a personal belief in your own ability and identity regardless of circumstances or people's opinions. Confidence, or as Todd White calls it, "Godfidence" is very important for leadership and speaking.

It's important to realize who we are, as most things in life flow from our identity. Sometimes it's good to even go through a sozo session (see Week 11), to remove any hurt or lies that were sewn into our hearts at young ages through lies or traumatic situations, and to hear and hold onto God's truth about ourselves moving forward. I went through a time in college where every time I asked the Holy Spirit about anything He would reply, 'just be confident', this happened over and over again until it was ingrained in me. Godly confidence is so important; remember, if you don't believe in yourself, it will be hard for others to believe in you or what you say.

Your Perspective about Your Identity

Your perspective about your identity is very important. Satan has spent so much time lying to us about who we are, it's very important for us to renew our mind to how God sees us.

The prodigal son had a wrong perspective on His identity. He thought His sin got in the way of His Father's love and said, "*I am now no longer worthy to be called my father side, but maybe he will take me back as a servant*" (Luke 15:19). We see that this perspective is wrong in contrast with how the father sees the son. When he was a long way off, his father runs to him and hugs him and instantly restores him to sonship with a robe and a feast.

We need to understand that much of our problem with identity and sonship is believing a lie based on things that we've done in the past.

1 John 1:9 says, "*If we confess our sins, God is faithful and just to cleanse us from all unrighteousness.*" We need to understand that God's love for us does not stop when we are sinning; He still loves us in the midst of the sin. He hates the sin but He loves us. The Bible says while we were yet sinners, Christ died for the ungodly (Romans 5:8).

We need to stop giving into condemnation, and letting it separate us from the love of the Father and from our true identity. <u>I believe that Satan's goal is not so much to get us to sin, as it is to get us to fall into the condemnation that can follow</u>. We need to let go of condemnation and turn from wrong-doing, and run to our Father because He is running to us with a robe and with a lineage of sonship that we could not imagine!

Do not be deceived into believing that you are a sinner; you are a son of God who may have sin inside of your flesh. God wants to cleanse it out of you and set you free. As a side note, if there is any addiction separating you from God, I would highly encourage you to start pursuing help in this area. God wants all His sons and daughters to live in complete freedom! Sometimes a focused program and/or live-in program for a bit is a good way to have some free mental space to seek God, and to get some forced isolation from the option of addiction.

B. Research, Activation, and Resources

Reading

 Bible - At least three chapters a day, beginning in Matthew.

 Textbook – The next Week

Watching

Art Montgomery - "Hey you! Do you want to be a Champion?"

https://www.youtube.com/watch?v=vcZho_oWSJY

Kris Vallotton - Your Identity as Sons of God

https://www.youtube.com/watch?v=GZtTSY889rA

Speaking

Commit to saying ten times a day: "I am a son of God. I am a champion. I am king. I am a priest. I am a new creation".

Doing

Decide in your heart to shift your perspective of yourself from a sinner, an addict, a wounded person, a broken person to that of a son/daughter of God, a king and a priest/queen and a priestess.

Passing

Assignments are due at the beginning of the following class.

☐ Have you asked God to be the main Father figure in your life and shifted your view from your natural dad as your father to your heavenly Father?

☐ Have you read the next Week in your workbook?

A. Teaching

God's love for us is unconditional, but it is very easy once you start moving in the supernatural to develop a performance mindset. What I mean by this is that we start to think that God's love for us is rated by how many people we heal, or deliver, or save. The error in this is that God's love started while you were still a sinner; it is impossible to earn that love after you get saved! This being said, many Christians fall into this performance mindset. Where they think that God's love for them is based on how they perform or what they do. Remember Mary and Martha. Martha expected Jesus to scold Mary because she was not working for Jesus. Martha thought Jesus's love for her was based on her serving him dinner and serving Him in general, but Jesus turns to Martha and says "*Martha you are worried about so many things, but Mary has chosen the better part*" (spending time with Jesus).

We often worry about God's love; that we're not doing enough to earn His love. But Jesus clearly said that Mary chose the better part. The crazy thing was she wasn't working at all, she was just sitting with Jesus and enjoying a relationship, and understanding that He loved her for who she was, not for what she did (Luke 10:38).

It is very important to understand that we are loved first. Romans 5:8 says, *"But God demonstrates His own love toward us, in that while we were still sinners, Christ died for us."* If God loved us while we were sinners, He doesn't stop once we get saved. That being said, the Bible is very clear about rewards in heaven: for fighting the good fight, saving souls, and being doers of the Word and not just hearers. Honestly, Western Christianity has become a "hearer's gospel", a gospel where people listen all the time and don't walk it out. Can you imagine if the millions of Christians in America actually were doers of the Word, healing, and delivering Holy Spirit power?

It is important to note that God's love for us is unconditional and not based on what we do. If we were to save fifty-nine people, heal 10,000 people, and raise forty people from the dead, God would still love us just the same. If you were a father and your son won a football game, you might be prouder of him, but the fatherly love you have for him would be there regardless of what he does or says. God's love for us is like this, unconditional and consistent.

A Side Note About Humility

Another big part of learning how to walk in God's power is to keep a heartset and a mindset of humility. Now I am not talking about getting religious and weird about it, we can fall into false humility where if every word doesn't sound humble, we walk in condemnation. We do need to know the balance of living in confidence and humility - to always give God the glory! Don't touch the glory! We see all throughout the bible when the disciples heal, they instantly point to Jesus! In Acts 3:12-16 Peter tells us, *"So when Peter saw it, he responded to the people: "Men of Israel, why do you marvel at this? Or why look so intently at us, as though by our own power or godliness we had made this man walk? The God of Abraham, Isaac, and Jacob, the God of our fathers, glorified His Servant Jesus, whom you delivered up and denied in the presence of Pilate, when he was determined to let Him go. But you denied the Holy One and the Just, and asked for a murderer to be granted to you, and killed the Prince of life (or the Originator), whom God raised from the dead, of which we are witnesses. And His name, through faith in His name, has made this man strong, whom you see and know. Yes, the faith which comes through Him has given him this perfect soundness in the presence of you all.*" Healing and miracles are an opportunity to first show the person God's love, and second, to create a moment in eternity of instant faith for the person to grasp the gospel and believe in God's plan for their lives! In John 3:30, John writes about Jesus that, *"He must increase, and I must decrease."* Jesus said, "*And I, if I am lifted up from the earth, will draw all peoples to Myself.*" (John 12:32). Don't get weird or religious with humility, choose to be humble and ask and trust God to perfect you in humility daily in your prayer and Word time and throughout your day. Remember to ALWAYS give God the glory, because it belongs to Him:)

Here's a great quote about humility from Oswald Chambers from his devotional, <u>My Utmost for His Highest</u>, November 16:

> *"Therefore, whether you eat or drink, or whatever you do, do all to the glory of God."*
> 1 Corinthians 10:31
>
> The great marvel of the Incarnation slips into ordinary childhood's life; the great marvel of the Transfiguration vanishes in the devil-possessed valley; the glory of the Resurrection descends into a breakfast by the seashore. This not an anti-climax, but a great revelation of God.
>
> The tendency to look for the marvelous in our experience; we mistake the sense of the heroic for being heroes. It is one thing to go through a crisis grandly, but another thing to go through every day glorifying God when there is no witness, no limelight, no one paying the remotest attention to us. If we do not want medieval haloes, we want something that will make people say – What a wonderful man of prayer he is! What a pious, devoted woman she is! If you are rightly devoted to the Lord Jesus, you have received the sublime height where no one ever thinks of noticing you; all that is noticed is that the power of God comes through you all the time.
>
> Oh, I have a wonderful call from God! It takes Almighty God Incarnate in us to do the meanest duty to the glory of God. It takes God's Spirit in us to make us so absolutely humanly His that we are utterly unnoticeable. The test of the life of the saint is not success, but faithfulness in life as it actually is. We will set up success in Christian work as the aim; the aim is to manifest the glory of God in human life, to live the life hid with Christ in God in human conditions. Our human relationships are the actual conditions in which the ideal life of God is to be exhibited.

B. Research, Activation, and Resources+

Reading

Bible - At least three chapters a day, Beginning in Matthew.

Textbook – Read the next Week

Watching

 Pete Cabrera Jr - "This is why I cry"

 https://www.youtube.com/watch?v=aeKJ596849g

Speaking

 Commit to saying ten times a day: "No matter what I do, where I go, who I am, God loves me and this love is not earned, it's because of who I am."

Doing

 Decide in your heart to shift your perspective of God's love to unconditional, that He loves you like a good Father, and no amount of performance can change that.

Passing

Assignments are due at the beginning of the following Class.

☐ Have you shifted your perspective of yourself from a sinner, an addict, a wounded person, a broken person to that of a son/daughter of God, a king and a priest/queen and a priestess?

☐ Right now, identify and write down how you used to think of yourself, and how you do now, according to God's/Your view of you.

_____

_____

_____

_____

_____

_____

_____

_____

_____

_____

☐ Have you read the next Week in your workbook?

Week 6 - Gifts: Healing on the Streets

This lady had fibromyalgia and all pain disappeared. This photo was taken a month later; these were all the medications she used to take for pain management!

A. Teaching

This Week, we are going to explore how to move in healing by faith, or in other words expectancy; not as a need or a gift for our general health, but as a tool to be used to preach the gospel. A great quote from Kenneth E. Hagin is that "healings are the dinner bell for salvations" and that is very true. Paul said, *"For Jews request a sign, and Greeks seek after wisdom;"* (1 Cor 1:22).

Another interesting point is that when Jesus called His disciples initially, He said "Come and I will make you fishers of men." To be a good fisher, you need the right bait. In another verse Paul says is *"I am all things to all men that I might win some"* (1 Cor 9:22). Jesus said, *"Behold, I send you out as sheep in the midst of wolves. Therefore be wise as serpents and harmless as doves."* (Matthew 10:16).

What we see is a consistent theme of catering to the desires of people to reveal Jesus to them. The end goal is not the miracle, the miracle is just bait for the fish, but too many people, especially in America, use it as "power bait." Jesus went as far to say to His generation that they wouldn't' even have sin if they didn't see the miracles that He did, but since they saw them (the bait,) and still don't' believe, now they have sin (John 10:37).

We see that for salvation, *"For Jews request a sign, and Greeks seek after wisdom;"* to believe that God is real (1 Cor 1:22). In Paul's journey to the Greeks, there are many hours not debating, but reasoning with them, and many got saved. However, on the day of Pentecost, when thousands of Jews got saved, it was because of the miracles of tongues (Acts 1 and 2). Therefore, we understand that for different peoples, there are different types of baits, but the two main ones are wisdom and miracles.

I would say that for the American people, since there is such a high focus on education and using the mind, the supernatural is an incredible tool for evangelism, because many times it helps Americans to stop trying to use their brain and logic and realize that there is a whole other world and realm out there.

The concept of the power of God increasing the effectiveness of evangelism is not just a theory, but this is something that we have applied on the streets and all over, and seen to be very, very effective in practice. When I first started doing evangelism, I was a student at UC San Diego and had somewhere in the ballpark of 300 conversations with people I tried to debate them into the kingdom. I used the four spiritual laws (this is a great and simple tract put out by Bill Bright's Ministry) and other spiritual surveys to try and talk them into the kingdom and to lead them to Jesus.

In two years, I saw one, maybe two, conversions. I believe that I was using the wrong bait and that many Americans are so brain trained that they need a supernatural experience to get out of their head, though believing without seeing is better. This is not wrong, remember that Jesus said His generation would not have sin if they hadn't seen the miracles and still chosen not to believe. It's just about using the right bait for the right fish.

Now that we go out with the power of God, we will see anywhere from twenty to forty people get saved each night. The trick is using the right bait. In Western Society there has been such a huge focus on education and using the brain that many people forget that there is a whole other segment of reality or dimension that we call the spiritual world or the supernatural; many really want to see that God is real through His Power. Praise God that just like the Jews of Jesus's time, we have the gospel of Mark 16, the gospel of power to bring them! But many times, we need to practice it, because it has become so forgotten by most people in the church for hundreds of years.

Therefore, one of the main reasons we are giving this school is to teach people the power of evangelism, to touch this generation with God's love, the gospel message and the power of God.

We start with healing. This Week, we will teach you how to lay your hands on the sick and watch them get healed. I am at a point where I see eight out of ten people who I pray for get healed. All of the people we have discipled see miracles all the time! Yesterday I heard that two of our guys went out to a rehab center and this man who was in a bike accident and had leg braces on for twenty years got prayed for and instantly healed. His legs got very hot and he shouted "get these things off of me'. When they took the braces off, he started walking without pain for the first time in twenty years. After that, they had fifty of the guys in the rehab come forward to get filled with the Holy Spirit. By the end of it, there were people speaking in tongues and on the ground everywhere. I would say I hear at least ten to twenty miracles a week from different people in our Church and community, and it keeps growing and growing. We were at the Chicano Park revival event and a deaf girl's ears had just opened up. I saw another man who was deaf and mostly mute; I said Jesus would heal him, and commanded the deafness to go. I didn't see any apparent change, but I decided to expect he was healed; sure enough he flagged me down in 10 minutes and said he could hear perfectly again and could talk as well! He was so excited:)! In the last two years, we've seen hundreds of people healed. Three weeks ago, we had three deaf ears open up. We saw people paralyzed with strokes healed. I personally saw a mute man who had had a stroke get completely healed, two dead people raised, a couple of blind eyes open and we're expecting for more. Of course, all these people who had miracles done to them got saved and filled on the spot! Wouldn't you?

We are now going to dive into the practical part of healing! Something we teach in all of our conferences is a basic six-step understanding of the miraculous. I would encourage you even though we have simplified it, to treat each point as a major revelation, for that is what it is. We have compiled this information from what we have seen work, and what other great men and women of God have seen. If you practice it consistently you will see incredible fruit! Remember, many times as Christians, we have stopped seeing the miraculous, because of how we have been taught. Many of the concepts in this book are to help combat what our western mindset of Christianity has become, and to allows us to get back to the basics of preaching the gospel of Jesus - preaching and miracles!

Basic Six-Step Understanding of The Miraculous

There are six basic steps to understand the miraculous. They are: expectancy, turning your natural brain off, our authority as believers, listening to Holy Spirit, Persistence - Wash, Rinse, Repeat, and Testing the healing:

1. Expectancy

First, be expectant. Jesus said, *"only believe, all things are possible only believe"* (Mark 5:36,9:23). Expectancy is a contemporary word that helps us wrap our minds around faith and belief. We need to expect a miracle, before we see it, before we even step onto the street. We read many stories where Jesus says, *"according to your faith be it done on to you;"* (Matthew 9:29). Expectancy or faith is a huge thing! Many times, this journey of healing has been learning that no matter what, we need to always have our expectancy turned on. We need to have full expectancy, and to choose to EXPECT from our hearts that: 100% of the people, 100% of the time, will get 100% healed the first time, and the problem will never come back! Our expectancy determines the consistency of our results for healing. The Holy Spirit will move sovereignly in healings and miracles, but if we want consistent results, we have to learn to expect the miracle before it happens.

When I am traveling to a healing, I shift my heart-set to be one of expectancy, and ask the Holy Spirit to show me and help me remove any doubts beforehand that have been collecting during the week. This is important. Jesus said *"For assuredly, I say to you, whoever says to this mountain, 'Be removed and be cast into the sea,' and does not doubt in his heart, but believes that those things he says will be done, he will have whatever he says. Therefore I say to you, whatever things you ask when you pray, believe that you receive them, and you will have them."*

(Mark 11:23-24). These are two separate things, we need to choose to believe from our heart or spirit, and not let doubts fester in our minds so they don't drop down into our spirits!

2. Turning Your Natural Brain Off

The second point is turning your brain off. Romans 8:7 says *"..the carnal mind is enmity against God; for it is not subject to the law of God, nor indeed can be."* Carnal is not bad in the Greek, just completely natural. Tom Loud really helped me understand this concept more. Many times, our naturally focused brain gets in the way of healing and the miraculous. In Western society, we have learned to overuse our brain for everything, including spiritual matters. Your brain is great for life, for logic, for confidence, and for basic living but when you die, it will decompose with your natural body. Your spirit, though, lives forever and will find its eternal destination in Heaven or Hell.

Therefore, we have to learn to stop trying to use our natural brain for spiritual things. Learning to not use my brain and to turn my brain off when I pray for people has made a HUGE difference. It's giving me a lot more boldness. Now I can pray for someone in the middle of the center aisle at Walmart or the mall, kneel down, and command people to get out of wheelchairs, and legs to grow, without having my natural mind freak out, take over and tell me to run!

When people ask me what I'm thinking about, I tell them absolutely nothing; my heart is expecting that they will get healed. Sometimes, I even choose to see their body part healed in my spirit. My natural brain is completely empty and not thinking about anything; I don't use it because that is not what it's for.

Choose to not think about anything or trying to will something to happen; just relax and let the Holy Spirit flow through you and heal them. In many verses we see power just going through Jesus.

If we become a vessel that God can use while staying in a relationship and then going out, we will be so filled that we need not try and force healings, they will flow out of us. In Luke 6:19, Jesus experienced that, *"...the whole multitude sought to touch Him, for power went out from Him and healed them all."* In Luke 8:46, Jesus said, *"Somebody touched Me, for I perceived power going out from Me."* We still need to renew our minds through the Word, but when healing people, sometimes it's easier to just not use our natural mind and let the Holy Spirit flow.

3. Our Authority as Believers

Another big thing is learning how to command, not request. Kenneth Hagin's book, The Believer's Authority has changed mine and millions of people's lives. We need to understand that we have full authority and dominion because of who we serve, because of who our Father is, and because of what Jesus did.

In Matthew 10:1 Jesus says, "*I give you all authority*" In Ephesians 1:20-21, Paul explains to the church of Ephesus, "*He raised Him from the dead and seated Him at His right hand in the heavenly places, far above all principality and power and might and dominion, and every name that is named, not only in this age but also in that which is to come.*" In Ephesians 2:6, Paul explains that we are "*raised us up together, and made us sit together in the heavenly places in Christ Jesus.*" Therefore, our position going into healing, deliverance, and raising the dead needs to be one of complete authority, and not requesting or begging God to do something. We can ask the Holy Spirit for insight or come boldly before God in our time of need, but mostly we need to use the authority that Jesus gave us already, instead of asking God to do everything. We have authority in Jesus name to cast out demons, authority to heal the sick, authority to raise the dead, authority to cleanse cancer. When we pray for people, I command the sickness to go, the demon to leave, I do not ask it to go, or ask God to do it, in the name of Jesus I have full authority over everything. If we go back to Genesis 1:26-28, in the very beginning, God made Adam to rule, and gave him dominion over everything. Our authority in Christ reinstates that authority and dominion to reign over everything through Jesus.

4. Listening to the Holy Spirit

We need to learn how to listen to the Holy Spirit. In a previous Week, we talked about learning to have a relationship with the Holy Spirit and learning to hear God's voice. It is important that we learn to hear the Holy Spirit, He speaks in a still voice on the inside, typically around our belly area.

In John 7:38, Jesus told the woman at the well that "*He that believeth on me, as the scripture hath said, out of his belly shall flow rivers of living water.*" (New King James translation quoted here.) Stop using your brain and drop down into your spirit and listen. Science shows us we have just as many, if not more, neuroreceptors in our stomach as we do our brain (Gut Feelings, <u>The Second Brain</u> by Michael D. Gershon, page 1). This means our stomach has the ability to receive signals and communication just like our brain. This is very important; guys we need to stop using our brains to try and hear God and drop down into our spirits and listen. 1 Kings 19:12-13 says, "*...but the Lord was not in the fire; and after the fire a still small voice. So it was, when Elijah heard it, that he wrapped his face in his mantle and went out and stood in the entrance of the cave. Suddenly a voice came to him, and said, "What are you doing here, Elijah?"*

Remember, we need to be able to drop our consciousness from our brain into our stomach (spirit) and listen to the Holy Spirit. Getting quiet normally helps. Many times, in a deliverance and healing, we might need some heavenly insight, and it may be good to stop and listen and see what the Holy Spirit is saying. Remember He is our Comforter. He is our God. He wants to lead us into all truth; we just have to trust him and listen and obey. Some of the craziest miracles I've ever heard come from just obeying the Holy Spirit's voice. If you get a chance to listen to Shawn Hurley on YouTube, he operates in creative miracles a lot and almost always, it has to do with listening to and obeying the Holy Spirit's voice.

5. Persistence - Wash, Rinse, Repeat

Repeat until healed, there's an interesting story in Mark 8:24, where Jesus is praying for a blind man, then He turns to the blind man and asked him how do you see? The blind man says I see men like trees walking. In other words, they were still blurry, so Jesus the son of God who has all power and authority, prayed two times, and then the man could see perfectly!

If Jesus has all power and authority, raised dead people, walked on water, why did He need to pray twice?

I think the simple answer may be that He wanted to show us that persistence is key. When He talks about prayer, He always talks about persistence and perseverance. The woman with the unjust judge, and the man waking up his neighbor at night (Luke 18:1-8, 11:5). Persistence is a key part of getting miracles and healing. I believe Jesus was not just talking about persevering in our vertical prayers to God, but also about persisting in our horizontal prayers for each other. With healing specifically, as long as the person is willing, don't give up until the job is done. Also, before you start praying for others' hurts, ask them on a scale of 1 to 10 how bad is your pain initially? This really helps with the persistence process; so even if the pain does not go away completely, you and they can watch it slowly go down and then leave. Always keep your expectancy that it will go away completely the first time.

We were in France on a mission trip at a Church, and my wife Lyd, prayed for a girl twelve times. She had a broken ankle and could not walk on it without pain. By the twelfth prayer, she was running around the Church at full speed; the pain was gone and her ankle was healed. The next day the girl showed up to Church without pain and with a great testimony! Remember though, if Lyd had not committed to seeing her healed and persevering through with her healing prayers, it would not have been possible.

There are two main reasons people don't get healed. In the healing process, considering these things is important:

The first reason, is a spirit needs to be cast out first and then the person will be able to receive their healing. We see a woman who Jesus casts a demon out of and she is healed. Jesus casts mute and dumb spirits out of people and they are instantly healed. Sometimes you need to deal with the demon first and the sickness will just go without a healing prayer, Jesus did this all the time (Luke 11:14, Luke 13:10-17). Sometimes however, getting the demon out actually allows the person to now effectively receive your prayer of healing for them. The three demons we see the most in accordance with healing are infirmity, trauma, and death. I encourage you, while praying for people, to use your authority, and tell any spirits of infirmity or trauma to leave people on your first prayer. If it's a mortal condition or you are raising the dead, always rebuke a spirit of death. Kenneth E. Hagin believed that any condition causing people to die prematurely was not in God's will and therefore should be contended for. Many times, you will need to rebuke a spirit of death when this is the case. In Hebrew the spirit of death was called Abaddon; in Greek it was called Apollyon (Strongs 11, Strongs 623).

Remember as a side note for deliverance, everyone has a different personality. Some of us are louder and some of us are quieter, but regardless of your personality, your authority is in your belief system and not necessarily your volume.

A quick story about Smith Wigglesworth to illustrate my point on how deliverance and healing many times go hand-in-hand. This excerpt is from his book entitled Ever Increasing Faith, chapter 2:

> At one time I was so bound that no human power could help me. My wife was looking for me to pass away. There was no help. At that time, I had just had a faint glimpse of Jesus as the Healer. For six months I had been suffering from appendicitis, occasionally getting temporary relief. I went to the mission of which I was pastor, but I was brought to the floor in awful agony, and they brought me home to my bed. All night I was praying, pleading for deliverance, but none came. My wife was sure it was my home call and sent for a physician. He said that there was no possible chance for me -- my body was too weak. Having had the appendicitis for six months, my whole system was drained, and, because of that, he thought that it was too late for an operation. He left my wife in a state of broken-heartedness.

> After he left, there came to our door a young man and an old lady. I knew that she was a woman of real prayer. They came upstairs to my room. This young man jumped on the bed and commanded the evil spirit to come out of me. He shouted, "Come out, you devil; I command you to come out in the name of Jesus!" There was no chance for an argument, or for me to tell him that I would never believe that there was a devil inside of me. The thing had to go in the name of Jesus, and it went, and I was instantly healed.

> I arose and dressed and went downstairs. I was still in the plumbing business, and I asked my wife, "Is there any work in? I am all right now, and I am going to work." I found there was a certain job to be done and I picked up my tools and went off to do it. Just after I left, the doctor came in, put his plug hat down in the hall, and walked up to the bedroom. But the invalid was not there. "Where is Mr. Wigglesworth? he asked. "O, doctor, he's gone out to work," said my wife. "You'll never see him alive again," said the doctor; "they'll bring him back a corpse." Well, I'm the corpse.

This is such a great story, because it highlights the fact that as a Christian, you can still have a demon try and live and cause damage in your body and second that the demon was the reason Smith was sick, it wasn't actually a stand-alone sickness. As soon as it got cast out, there was no recorded healing prayer, but Smith was just instantly healed! (I do not believe a follower of Jesus can be possessed in their spirit, but just like diseases still try and attack christians' bodies, I believe demons will try as well.)

The Second reason people don't get healed is that the person needs to forgive someone! Unforgiveness is the only sin I have seen get in the way of a healing, it is very rare, but I do see it. Probably one in twenty people need to forgive before we see an instant healing. This is the only thing other than a spirit I have ever seen block a healing. I normally expect they are 100% ready when I start. Most times, the Holy Spirit shows me and they confirm that they need to forgive someone, it's not something I assume. Whenever people asked Jesus about healing, He would always relay it back to belief or unbelief. I believe this solves for 99% of most healings. Most times, people aren't getting healed because we don't have the expectancy to persist through and heal them:)

6. *Testing the Healing*

Many times in the past, the church has said to heal by blind faith only, and that testing it out afterward is a form of doubt. This is not the case. Jesus told many people who were healed to go and have the Pharisees check them out (Luke 17:14). Confirming a healing for a miracle, gives the person the ability to activate their own faith through action. It also adds integrity to the healing, instead of just having the person believe they are healed only because of the words you speak.

With testing out the healing on the spot, use a lot of wisdom. Try and only do what the person is comfortable with; if they have any type of injury on her leg, give them physical support. Make sure 100%, that you have their genuine verbal permission to test it out (it's good to have another person there to hear them say it as well). I encourage people before you do this, to make sure the pain has already left or is going down a lot. This is an important step. Just use wisdom, and don't rush into it. Every situation and every person is completely different. I like to see many major miracles happen ONLY when people test out the injury. Imagine if you were Peter and John in Acts 3:1-8, would the lame man have walked if Peter hadn't helped him up? Use wisdom and ask for permission, but on-the -spot testing is a big part of healings.

What If It Comes Back?

Ok, this is one of my favorite questions. To start this, we need to understand the progression of faith and expectancy in the contemporary church in America. In my experience, the church in America as a whole does not see many healings and miracles, and has a very low threshold for this when first starting out, so we have to ease them into it!

The First Lie

The first lie that is in our natural mind is that "no-one will get healed". To pray for people, we have to overcome this lie and move forward into setting the captives free. The biggest way to do this is choosing to expect in your heart that: 100% of the people, 100% of the time, will get 100% healed. Do not allow doubt to permeate your heart or mind. As you pray for people you will start to see them getting healed. As this happens, since Satan couldn't get them with the first lie, he will try with the second lie.

The Second Lie

The second lie is that when you pray, people's pain will go down, but it won't leave completely. This is a lie and we need to just believe that 100% of the people, 100% of the time, will get 100% healed; let that be our expectancy before and during prayer for people. If you believe that they will fully recover, it will happen!

The Third Lie

The third lie is meant to stop your expectation from finishing the work that God has begun in their lives. The third lie says, "sure they got healed, but it will come back on them." This is a lie, and is another form of doubt. The enemy is trying to get you to side with his reality of doubt and destruction again. If he couldn't' stop your expectancy from getting them healed, he will try and get you to side with a lie in your heart that they won't stay healed.

The Truth

Many people who get healed in the moment, have never been pain-free from that injury since it started, and therefore it is an actual, genuine miracle that they are pain-free. So, the same God who has the power to take their pain away temporarily has the power to take it away for good. and According to Matthew 10:1, *"And when He had called unto him his twelve disciples, He gave them power against unclean spirits, to cast them out, and to heal all manner of sickness and all manner of disease."* In Mark 16:15-18, that power has been delegated over to you. *"Go ye into all the world, and preach the gospel to every creature. He that believeth and is baptized shall be saved; but he that believeth not shall be damned. And these signs shall follow them that believe; In my name shall they cast out devils; they shall speak with new tongues; They shall take up serpents; and if they drink any deadly thing, it shall not hurt them; they shall lay hands on the sick, and they shall recover."*

Your expectancy just needs to line up with this truth. Jesus knew this; He said in Mark 9:25 *"Thou dumb and deaf spirit, I charge thee, come out of him, and enter no more into him."*

I believe in healing someone by setting my expectancy and commanding the sickness or demon to leave and never come back. If God has the power to temporarily kick out a sickness, He has the power to ultimately kick out the sickness; the question is, (remember this phrase) <u>what are you going to believe after you leave</u>? Remember, *"According to your faith be it unto you"* (Mark 9:29). After you pray for them and you leave, set your expectation that it will never come back. Don't side with the doubt from your natural mind that may try and creep in. I would even say, if there is a doubt like that trying to persist in your mind, <u>with your heart choose to believe</u> that they will never lose that healing. Every time it pops in your mind, DECLARE OUT LOUD that THEY WILL STAY HEALED and IT WILL NEVER COME BACK ON THEM.

My Experience

I started praying for people and no one got healed right away, but when I started to see people get partially healed and the scale of pain going down, then they would get all the way healed. I was afraid for the first six months that it would come back on them...until one day.

I had been leading worship downtown at this little Church called International House of Love for the homeless people in San Diego Lydia and I had just started to operate in faith and healing; people were getting healed like crazy. This was huge for me because although I grew up believing in miracles and had prayed for people, I had never seen others really get healed by my prayers. Secretly I had this fear that in some people, the pain was just going to come back on them when they left. There was this lady, Elaine, who had come in, super sweet, she was in her 80s. Her shoulder was messed up and she couldn't raise her hands. I prayed for her and she was healed instantly. The full range of motion was restored and with no pain. It was one of the bigger miracles I had seen at that time, but for that night and for the rest of the week, I was so afraid that the pain would come back to her.

I saw her two weeks later and she had a sling on her arm again. I was so dejected and sad; my natural mind was saying, "what I was afraid of is true". The meeting ended and I prayed for her for a very short time. I believed the lie, and therefore was so disheartened I just left.

At that point we had some other things happening in our lives and we didn't get back out to the Church for a while. Finally, when I went back in two months, I saw Elaine again and guess what?

She wasn't wearing the sling, and said that she had had no pain since we prayed for her the second time and her arm was completely healed.

Consequently, I had a massive revelation. I had let the thief steal the joy of God's victory by listening to my natural mind about spiritual matters. From then on, I <u>decided in my heart to believe</u> and pray that people will get healed, and that the spirit of sickness will never return to them. Lastly, I decided to always set my heart on an expectation for full healing initially and ultimately.

As a side note, if the person goes back into a lifestyle of sin that invites other sicknesses, that's their choice. But my choice is to believe that no matter what, no matter when, no matter what they do, they will stay healed. I always believe that 100% of the people, 100% of the time, will get 100% healed! Remember Jesus said to simply believe; it's not hard, we just need to be intentional about our expectancy.

Before you Heal the Streets

A couple things to know before you go. These will change your outreach, from a polite group of people kick-starting themselves in the gifts, to a band of warriors and a Joel 2 army, who fulfill the Lord's prayer by bringing the Kingdom of Heaven to Earth. We are not just called to be polite Christians, who fit perfectly into the boxes of society that humanism and political correctness have constructed for us, we are called to CHANGE THE WORLD! *"These that have turned the world upside down are come here also."* (Acts 17:6).

OUTREACH TIP 1

This goes hand-in-hand with this prayer Week, but one of the biggest things I ever learned was to pray in the Spirit for thirty minutes before we go out on the street; tell the fallen god of this world to take his hands off of people's eyes and ears so they can receive the gospel. 2 Corinthians 4:4 says, *"whose minds the god of this age has blinded, who do not believe, lest the light of the gospel of the glory of Christ, who is the image of God, should shine on them."* When I first went out, I would see little miracles here and there, but when I started praying beforehand, there was such a strong flow and function all over outreach, everyone would get lit up with God's power; there was always a very strong flow of revival power everywhere we went. We have started saying on the streets that you need to pray it out before you play it out.

I want to talk with you briefly about the term that we have coined in our ministry called "Holy Spirit Acceleration". This term simply means to have Holy Spirit take over while you are moving in the gifts and take control of the situation. Holy Spirit acceleration is the concept you have been waiting for; you may not know it yet, but this is the trick to change your outreach. Remember, He is the Spirit of God and is a gentleman, so He will not take control unless you first invite Him, and second, let go of the reigns. Practically it looks like this:

- Pray for about 15-20 minutes beforehand,
- Start to feel Him move

> it could be an impression to pray for a specific person,
>
> or to go a specific direction,
>
> or to start talking about something you wouldn't normally talk about,
>
> or to have specific insight into people's lives that you could not know naturally

when any of these happen, you just go with it and trust God, because this will allow His Spirit to start to move. It is so important to be building relationships with the Holy Spirit during this whole process and get to know Him. Many people are growing in the gifts, but not many people are growing in the Holy Spirit Acceleration of those gifts. At first, the disciples were moving in the gifts with very little personal change, but when they combined active, thriving, teaching, communication and partnership from Holy Spirit, everything changed. I MEAN EVERYTHING. SO MUCH SO THAT EVEN PETER'S SHADOW HEALED PEOPLE (Acts 5:15).

Here's what you need to start doing. Before your outreach, during prayer, say these words - "HOLY SPIRIT TAKE OVER THIS OUTREACH. HOLY SPIRIT DO WHAT YOU WANT TONIGHT. HOLY SPIRIT MOVE HOW YOU WANT TO TONIGHT." THEN BE READY TO LET GO OF CONTROL, BECAUSE IT'S ABOUT TO GET REAL.

Ephesians 5:18 says *"And do not get drunk with wine, for that is debauchery; but ever be filled and stimulated with the [Holy] Spirit."* On a side note, many times getting filled with the Holy Spirit, like in Acts 2:15 will seem like you are a little drunk; that's ok, in the same way people call alcohol "liquid courage." The boldness of the Holy Spirit comes when you let go of the fear of how you look; learn to just get filled with His Presence and stay drunk in the Holy Spirit. This is not for the sake of looking foolish, but for the sake of letting go of your fear of man. Only then can you really do everything that God puts in front of you!

The Bible says be not drunk with wine, but be filled with the Holy Spirit. BEFORE YOU GO OUT, GET FILLED WITH HIS GLORY until you overflow. Then minister out of overflow! When you learn to minister out of the overflow of the power of the Holy Spirit, you will change the world.

This is what happened in Acts 2. They were filled with Holy Spirit and then they ministered out of the overflow with boldness, and thousands got saved the first day. The crazy thing is, the same bunch of disciples all got filled again in Acts 4, and the direct result was evangelizing with boldness. "*And when they had prayed, the place was shaken where they were assembled together; and they were all filled with the Holy Ghost, and they spoke the Word of God with boldness*" (Acts 4:31).

Learn to get filled to overflowing before you hit the streets and it will feel like you are going out in a river. No matter how dark or evil the area is, the Holy Spirit will flow down and you will be filled with power and boldness to take this Jesus to the whole world with Fiyah.

A practical way to do this, is start praying for each other before you go out, pray for an increase of Anointing and more Holy Spirit on each person before you go out. Stir each other up in the Holy Spirit. Hebrews 10:24-25 says, "*And let us consider one another in order to stir up love and good works, not forsaking the assembling of ourselves together, as is the manner of some, but exhorting one another, and so much the more as you see the Day approaching.*" Also watch videos of Holy Spirit laughter meetings over and over again, like the Old Kenneth Hagin Holy Spirit Laughter videos, this will get you filled up. At Rhema they always say, "the anointing is caught not taught".

B. Research, Activation, and Resources

Reading
> **Bible** - At least three chapters a day, beginning in Matthew. Meditate on all healings in Matthew 8 and 9.
>
> **Textbook**- – Read the next Week
>
> **Required Reading -** Ever Increasing Faith, Smith Wigglesworth

Suggested Reading – Book of Joel, Chapter 2

Watching:

1.Tom Loud - "Unlocking Kingdom Power" (Classes 1-5)

https://www.youtube.com/watch?v=P7zgFXmWhjQ&t=1s

2. Church Tsidkenu - Deaf Girl Healed in Jesus Name!

https://www.youtube.com/watch?v=Hh72fMRE5qM

3. Art Montgomery - FREED FROM THE DEMON WHEEL CHAIR

https://www.youtube.com/watch?v=w2xDkBuNGxs

4. Kenneth Hagin - 1997/10/14 St Louis Holy Ghost Meeting

https://www.youtube.com/watch?v=WGr7E-Y0kCE&t=824s

5. Shawn Hurley - They Were All Healed

https://www.youtube.com/watch?v=3uCSlybCf8I&t=85s

Speaking

Commit to saying ten times a day: "No matter what I do or where I go, God loves me, and this love is not earned, it's because of who I am."

Doing:

1.   **Be Expectant** - decide to expect FROM YOUR HEART/SPIRIT the miracle before you start praying. (Mark 11:24)

2.   **Turn your brain off** - your natural, educated brain will fight against the Holy Spirit. Choose to not think anything while you're praying. (Romans 8:7)

3.   **Command, don't request** - all authority has been given to you by Jesus; commanding activates that authority. (Matt 10:1, Phil 2:10, Matt 8:8-10)

4.   **Listen to the Holy Spirit** - stop and just listen, especially if you're not seeing the result you want.

5.   **Repeat till Healed** - be okay with praying multiple times. Start by commanding injury to be healed, and any spirits of infirmity or trauma to go (Matthew 8:24).

6.   **TEST IT OUT** - if you can, get them to activate their own faith by moving the area that needed healing, MOST healings will happen instantly while this is happening. Be wise about this and don't' force people to do something they don't want to.

Passing

Assignments are due at the beginning of the following class.

☐ Have you identified and written down how you used to think of yourself and how you do now, according to God's/your view of you?

_____

_____

_____

_____

_____

_____

_____

_____

_____

_____

_____

_____

_____

_____

☐ Have you read the next Week in your workbook?

☐ Have you read the Word, and made time to pray this past week?

Week 7 - Gifts: Healing Yourself

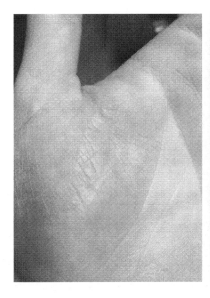
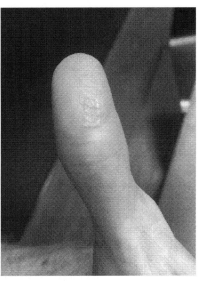

A. Teaching

It's very important for the believer to learn how to live in divine healing. Kenneth Hagin talks about not having so much as a cold for 40 years while ministering. I know for myself, I have been healed instantly of many, many things - my rotator cuff two different times, my knee restored, my back, fevers, among probably about 60 different big and little personal physical problems. One time I was on a camping trip when Church Tsidkenu had just started, I grabbed a pan out of the fire and severely burned my hand. I instantly knew I had to get away and pray, so I withdrew from everyone and prayed for my hand, not allowing the thoughts of doubt or trauma to have a resting place in my mind. I would normally have had pain all over my hand for a burn half as bad, and be putting butter and toothpaste on it all day; not this time, I had complete healing. Right before we went hiking for whole day, a thought of doubt came into my head and said, "your hand will start hurting and you will have to turn back and everyone will know this is not real." as soon as that thought came, I felt pain for the first time from the burn trying to come in. I didn't let the thought sit in my mind, but laughed and thanked God I was healed. It left and so did the pain and I never felt it again. Also, my burn scars disappeared in a couple weeks.

Here are a couple pictures of the burn; you can see where the skin is seared, but zero pain and scars disappeared.

As a side story on that, a woman, new to our Church, called me after leaving the ER and they couldn't do anything for her, she had fallen asleep on the beach and got horrible sunburns all over her body. She called me sobbing saying she was in horrible 10/10 pain level and was allergic to the pain medications at the ER, and therefore had no medical help. I told her the pain would leave when we prayed, and it did. I saw her a few days later; it had not come back! We have to understand that healing is part of the covenant, and what Christ purchased for us. In first Peter 2:24, we understand that by the whip marks on Jesus stripes, He bought our forgiveness and freedom from sickness. We also see this in Deuteronomy 28, where it talks about the curses for disobeying the law and the blessings for obeying the law. If the new law is fulfilled by our faith in Jesus, then our forgiveness and our healing comes by the same faith (1 Peter 2:24, Isaiah 53:3-5, Deuteronomy 29).

I would also encourage you to look up the words from Isaiah 53:4 in the original Hebrew. First, the word 'sorrows' is mistranslated and in the Hebrew. The word is makob and actually means pains, second is griefs, this is the word Choli in the Hebrew and actually means sicknesses (Strongs 2483, & 4341).

Isaiah should read like this: "Surely He hath borne our **sicknesses**, and carried our **pains**: yet we did esteem him stricken, smitten of God, and afflicted." Jesus paid for our sin AND our sickness on the cross, we need not pay twice for something He already paid for, now we just need to take it and appropriate it with our "hands of faith." In John 15, Jesus says, *"if you abide in Me then He will ask whatever you desire, and my Father will give it to you."*

I don't think spending time with God changes His giving heart toward us, I think spending time with God gives us the ability to know Him and expect from Him without our nature getting in the way. Therefore, a large part of receiving our personal healing is learning how to spend time with God daily in His Word and in prayer (John 15).

Abiding in the Word

Romans 10:17 says, "faith comes by hearing and hearing by the Word of God." Therefore, as we read the Word of God especially out loud, faith will start to rise up for our healing, and it will be much easier to walk in divine healing, and pray for that healing. Kenneth Hagin senior raised himself off the deathbed by simply reading his grandmother's Bible. We are robbed of many things because we are not in the Word. Hosea 4:6 says, "my people perish for the lack of knowledge;" knowledge comes from the Word. Especially for personal healing we need to live in the Word of God daily and meditate on healing scriptures daily; spend 10 minutes on one healing verse, reading it out loud over and over. I also recommend to listening to old Kenneth E. Hagin or Oral Roberts teachings on healing; you will feel your faith rise just listening to them!

Abiding in Healing Others

The Bible says that those who hear the Word of God and do it are the ones who are built on a good foundation. It's very important that we learn to be doers of the Word of God. Much faith for personal healing comes from praying for others and seeing them get healed. As we heal others, our personal faith arises and it's easy to ward off sickness.

I encourage people to live in the lifestyle of praying for other people, as it increases their personal faith for them and their family for healing. I did not see any immediate healing for my family members until I started practicing and going on the streets and doing the great commission, now it's almost always instantaneous because I always stay in practice. I try and go out praying for people officially at least once a week to stay in practice.

IMPORTANT

Just like a public speech or a football game, if we aren't practicing healing, our faith muscles aren't working, so when it comes time to see a healing in us or our family, we are not ready and don't' know what to do or how to see a miracle. However, if we are practiced by doing the great commission, we are ready to go! If healing others becomes normal in our lives, seeing ourselves healed will as well!

The Bible says at least three times to just shall live by faith. We need to be practiced up with living through a faith mindset. Like it talks about in Ephesians, above all take the shield of faith. If we take that shield of faith, a.k.a. a faith mindset, and live with that when something attacks us, we are already on the offensive, so any defensive action will fall to the ground (Ephesians 6:16). I cannot tell you how many times since I've started praying for people, I've felt a scratching in the back of my throat, or had a headache trying to come on, or a cramp, or a sharp pain. Every time, I choose in my heart to believe with everything I have that I'm completely healed. The pain always leaves, and almost always instantly. We need to learn to live by faith. As soon as the thought of pain or hurt, or a trauma happens to us, we can first take it captive, not let fear or doubts in our mind, then choose to believe in our heart that the area of our body is healed (I like to visually picture and expect 100% that it is healed.) Then just stand on God's truth, and repeat this process multiple times till you see the healing. Lastly, again, don't forget to meditate in the Word of God daily.

B. Research, Activation, and Resources

Reading

Bible - At least three chapters a day, beginning in Matthew (meditate on healing stories)

Textbook - Read the next Week

Required Reading: Christ the Healer!, F.F. Bosworth

Suggested Reading: Jesus the Healer, E.W. Kenyon

Watching:

Kenneth Hagin - Healing, How to Receive it and Keep it!

https://www.youtube.com/watch?v=oAUaHqGA1Zc&t=1440s

Church Tsidkenu - Hernia Disappears in Jesus Name!

https://www.youtube.com/watch?v=3ap8pduTdww

Speaking

Commit to saying ten times a day: "Jesus paid for my health with the whip marks on His back and I walk in perfect health."

Doing

Decide in your heart to shift your perspective toward 100% healing. In the Bible, Jesus came to display the perfect will of God. He healed everyone who came to Him; it's God's perfect will for you to be healed 100% of the time.

The instant you feel some pain, sore throat, stomach ache, etc. capture the thought, realize it's an attack, rebuke it and start to believe you are healed WITH YOUR SPIRIT, NOT YOUR MIND.

Passing

Assignments are due at the beginning of the following class.

☐ Have you healed one to three people this past week? Please Explain.

_____

_____

_____

_____

_____

_____

_____

_____

_____

_____

_____

☐ Have you read the next Week in your workbook?

☐ Have you read and finished <u>Ever Increasing Faith</u>?

Week 8 - Gifts: Delivering Yourself

A. Teaching

As Christians, we need to be praying and reading the Word daily to renew our mind, break off attacks and build that relationship with God. However, if something is irritating you, and you are already praying and reading God's Word daily, but you still feel overpowered by a sin or a lie, many times it's a spirit or demon at the root and needs to be cast out (Romans 6:16, Mark 16:15-20, 1 Corinthians 6:12). I cannot stress abiding in God for self-deliverance enough! This is one of the biggest keys. Not abiding is the biggest reasons that so many people walking around incredibly oppressed.

I was talking to my friend who is a Ph.D. in psychology and had his own Christian counseling firm. He said, 'Ben if I told you what a high percentage of people were walking around with clinical psychosis, it would freak you out.' I do not doubt it at all.

Many times, people are very oppressed just going through life. This is how we explain it; we live in a fallen world and natural gravity is against us, my mantle at home collects dust just by sitting there. Just by being here, many times oppression and demonic stuff will try and sit on us. This does not even count for the people around us who might be misusing their powerful speech or giving into stuff they shouldn't be - the wrong type of television, allowing angry words, etc. I say all this to stress the importance of abiding with the right Spirit; because there are other spirits in our day-to-day, that are fighting for control.

Almost everyone had or has had a familiar spirit/demon at some point in their life. This is a secret area or sin in a person's life that people will habitually give in to, and run to, typically for comfort and rest, instead of running to God. Many times, it is secretly trying to convince you that it is part of your identity. The promise is complete rest and comfort in hard times of trauma or confusion; the truth is you keep giving up more freedom for this synthetic peace. There is one thing, one sin or lie, you keep going back to, and more often than not, it is been there most of your life. I would encourage you to ask the Holy Spirit what familiar spirit has been trying to live with you, and do some self-deliverance against it, and start renewing your mind to the truth of God's Word.

Mine was pornography, lust and an unhealthy addiction to beauty. These things tried to destroy my life. I remember at a very young age having something come into my life and slowly take over until it affected almost every area of my life. This was a spirit of lust and perversion. This thing lied to me and said: "it's normal, it's part of you, because of this you can't fight it". After years of seeking God for freedom and praying a lot and reading, I learned about deliverance and that this thing was not an actual part of me, it was a foreign (though initially it felt so familiar) presence trying to dominate my life and control me. I did some self-deliverance and it left and I have been free ever since. We need deliverance to get things out of our lives that aren't ours.

Find out what the familiar spirit that has been trying to control your life is, deal with that, and ask the Holy Spirit to replace its role in your life.

A Few Different Types of Self Deliverance

Praying in tongues is a direct form of self-deliverance. Most people will start to speak in tongues after they get baptized in the Holy Spirit and Fire. If the tongues don't flow out right away, take the initiative and start speaking in tongues by faith and it will stir up the River and then the Holy Spirit will take over. Jesus said in John 7:38, "*He who believes in Me, as the*

Scripture has said, out of his heart will flow rivers of living water." There are many prophetic texts in the Old Testament talking about the Holy Spirit as a river.

When you're praying in tongues, you are stirring up the gift that is inside of you. When the river starts flowing as you pray in tongues, many times, just as if water was spraying out of a pipe in the ground, it will wash all of the impurities out of the pipe on its way out (physical manifestations during this are pretty normal, throwing up, coughing, hearing lying voices, etc.) I encourage people to live a life where they walk in the Spirit through praying in tongues for at least twenty minutes a day. I personally pray for one to two hours every day in tongues, and it has changed my whole life! In the context of self-deliverance there's nothing more powerful than praying in tongues. As you do this, stuff will start to leave you and you'll start to feel light and free. The Holy Spirit will start to fill you up even more. Ephesians 5:19 says, "*...speaking to one another in psalms and hymns and spiritual songs, singing and making melody in your heart to the Lord...*" 2 Timothy 1:6-7 says, "*Therefore I remind you to stir up the gift of God which is in you through the laying on of my hands. For God hath not given us the spirit of fear; but of power, and of love, and of a sound mind.*"

Reading the Word

John 8:32 says, "you will know the truth and the truth will make you free;" staying in the Word is so important for deliverance. I would venture to say, this is the most important tool for self-deliverance. A lot of the need for deliverance and the fall into depression, is because of believing a lie. Romans 12:2 says to "*be transformed by the renewing of your mind.*" As you get in the Word, your mind will become renewed and you will experience incredible, incredible self-deliverance. You will be replacing the lies with truth. And He will be transforming your body. James 1:21 says that the Word has the power to save your souls. It's important to note that we are not just supposed to be eating the Word, or getting in the Word, we are supposed to be becoming the Word. Todd White says, "in the beginning was the Word and the Word became flesh and blood among us, so that our flesh could become Word".

Getting in the Word of God is not just about listening or hearing, it's about transforming your mind, and your body to become the living Word. Remember who is the Word? It's Jesus. The more we become like the Word the more we become like Him.

Speaking the Word

A huge part of reading the Word is speaking the Word. I personally read the Bible out loud. Romans 10:17 says that faith comes by hearing and hearing by the Word of God. I like to hear it with my ears. When you start making confessions this will change your whole life. It's so important to speak the truth of God's Word over your life.

If you struggle with condemnation, say ten times every day, "I am free from all condemnation and guilt and I walk in complete grace because of Jesus and not because of me." If you struggle with anger. Speak God's truth about it. James 1:19 says to be slow to anger; so say, "I am slow to anger, I am quick to forgive." Keep speaking this over your life until you are completely free. Renewing your mind is reading the Word with your eyes, but a huge part of it is also speaking the Word with your lips.

The Theory Behind the Actual Process for Self-Deliverance

Here is a great process for self-deliverance, in this paragraph we will be identifying a great process for self -deliverance. This first part is not for application, but is the theology and the theory behind self-deliverance. A bit farther down in the doing part we have created an actual step-by-step hands-on process for deliverance.

Initially you will want to identify the lie or trauma. Go through the inventory list at the end of the Week above, to see what the strongman might be in your case. See if you identify with a major loss of control, sin or hurt in any of those areas. You may need to pray and meditate on these, asking God to help you bring out the truth for you.

Next, you want to denounce the lie, or ask Jesus to heal you from the trauma; ask Jesus to show up in the trauma of that memory. Whatever lie you started believing right then, denounce it as a lie and not true. Combined with this, you will want to confess your sins, and turn from anything that you might've done wrong, or believed was a lie.

Believe the truth of God's Word. Many times, when the lie comes in, the best way to deal with it is choosing to believe the truth of God's Word. For example, you've struggled with rejection, and feel like people are rejecting you, choose to believe that since God accepts you, it is not possible to be really rejected by man; even if you are, it doesn't matter, so there should be no trauma. Honestly, many times the thought that people are rejecting you is a LIE and needs to be replaced with truth.

After that, you need to get aggressive and kick the demon out. You have all authority; you know what the lie is. Now it's time to kick the thing out of your life. Remember that Matthew 10:1 says you have all authority. Go after it. I personally like to do mirror deliverances on myself, because I enjoyed looking into my eyes and taking my authority over anything I see.

Lastly, it's so important that you are affirming yourself and your identity as a son of God! Do not focus on the demon, but rejoice for the freedom, and for what God has done for you.

B. Research, Activation, and Resources

Reading

Bible - At least three chapters a day, beginning in Matthew.

Textbook – Read the next Week

Watching:

Art Montgomery - "Get Deliverance Now. Powerful Interactive Video"

https://www.youtube.com/watch?v=0ap8Imvpc7k

Art Montgomery - HOW TO DO HEALING, SPEAK IN TONGUES AND DO DELIVERANCE

https://www.youtube.com/watch?v=lJNow1Qrdec

Speaking:

Say ten times a day, "I am free from all demonic strongholds, and no attack against my body will prosper."

Doing

Perform one to three deliverances on yourself.

Here is the actual hands-on, step-by-step process that goes along with the theory and theology on deliverance. If you are confused about where to start, go through the Deliverance Inventory at the end of this Week.

1. **Decide that you are a son or daughter of God, and that any sin that has tried to persist in your life is not part of your identity. You are a warrior and a champion.**

2. **How to Self-Deliver and Confess!**

a. **Where is there a loss of control, sin or oppression, when did it start?** (Romans 6:16). Each time you invite a demon back through sin or believing a lie, you must kick it out again (Luke 11:25).

Example: If it's fear, when do you first remember feeling afraid?

b. **REPENT and turn away from any sin involved, and denounce the lie you believed, and break agreement.**

Example: "I'm sorry for not believing God would protect me, and in Jesus name I denounce a spirit of fear."

c. **Cast the demon out with authority!** (Matthew 10:1, Matthew 8:16)

Example: "In Jesus name, I command you demon to leave."

Sometimes doing a deliverance in the mirror is easier.

d. **If the demon is lingering, command more (Holy Spirit) Fire on that area of your body.**

e. **Repeat till you feel release.**

f. Ask your Father for gifts and receive affirmation that you ARE a son or daughter of God and HE LOVES YOU SO MUCH.

Passing

Assignments are due at the beginning of the following class.

☐ Have you performed one to three deliverances on the street with you leading and been involved in two others this next week. Please explain _____

_____

_____

☐ Have you read the next Week in your workbook?

☐ Have you read and finished Pigs in the Parlor?

☐ Have you chosen to set aside time this week for quiet time and reading and praying? Please expound _____

_____

_____

_____

Deliverance Inventory
(this will also be used in the next 2 Weeks)

Root, Spirit/ Demon Name	Spiritual Inventory: Chronic Problems, Potential Signs of Oppression (Symptoms)
Death/Suicide	Spirit of death: mortal conditions, involvement in paganistic worship of or celebrations of death dark holidays, heart attack, cancer, actually physically dead, on their deathbed, and hospice. Suicidal thoughts, homicidal thoughts.
Jezebel	Manipulation and control. Must be control of all areas and people in an environment, distorts truth, always makes others seem in wrong, uses guilt as a tactic, normally mocks and scoffs at authority, will normally start to laugh as soon as confronted. Gravitates towards those with power and influence and will try and control them. Hangs out with people with religious spirits a lot.
Offense/ Unforgiveness	Won't forgive anyone, holds grudges, lots of bitterness, gets mad when talking about specific people, situations from past, won't forgive offense (sometimes cancer is associated with unforgiveness), mad, holding grudges, hard heart.
Terror/Fear	Nightmares or reoccurring terror intimidation, all phobias, shyness or inferiority, fear of failure, authority, loss of control, rejection, worry, anxiety, heart, disappointing others, stress, people; people pleasing.
Laziness/Sloth	Laziness, sloth, constant fatigue, lethargy, lack of focus, procrastination, chronic tardiness, passionless, chronic apathy, consistent quitting, lack of organization, withdrawn, satisfied being alone and without. Isolation.
Deaf, Blind, Mute Spirit	Disease of the eyes and/or ears deafness, chronic ear pain/ringing in the ears, muteness, attack on voice.
Pride	Talk about themselves, put others down, always have to have best story, one up everyone, deep down very insecure, arrogant, aloof, not willing to submit, always has to be right, looks down on others, compares themselves, talks a lot, listens little.
Depression/ Despair	Sad countenance, suicidal thoughts, fear of failure, massive apathy, sadness, hopelessness, despair, negative personal view, negative outlook on life. Given up on life. Given up on people. Too into media and movies. Escapism.

Confusion	Won't stop talking. Always needs to talk over you. Conversation doesn't make sense. Occultism, mixing and matching religions, talks about "morningstar"*, one of the big signs is pride and inflated ego, "I am the greatest", talks a lot about angels and non-biblical revelations, paranoia, fear of man, can't think straight, talks a lot but says little that makes sense.
Jealousy	Someone is always better than them in their mind, anger at others promotions or at others' fortunes in life, can't really enjoy others getting blessed, always looking at others, hard time receiving love from God, orphan complex, sometimes rejection as well. Poor self-image.
Infirmity or Sickness	All disease and sickness, especially things that have been around for a while. Cancer, diabetes, MS, overall feeling of despair, moving symptoms, when you pray they move around, when you pray for healing, nothing happens. Most sickness is demonic in nature, if they are not getting healed, cast the demon out. Jesus would often cast out demons and not pray for people and they would get healed.
Witchcraft/Occult	A constant feeling of heightened oppression no matter what you do. Talisman, Ouija boards, satanic, cartel rituals, witchcraft, mysticism, fortune tellers, tarot cards, and relationships with people who have done these; astrology, horoscopes, whispering spirits. Calling on spirit other than God, Satanic worship, shamans. Many time schizophrenics and multiple personalities disorders have these. Most extra voices you hear are demonic.
Religious or Anti-Christ	Offense, nit-picking on every detail, condemnation, anger outbursts, a lack of the ability to walk in love, more worried about being right than live, pride is very big here, major fear, will always act up when Holy Spirit is moving, hates Holy Spirit joy and any loss of control, confusing interpretation of scripture and always out of context. Sounds wise but is always out of context with the rest of the bible. Struggles with grace. Self-condemnation is very big for this spirit. Hard on themselves. Confusion. Typically, is influenced by a counterfeit Holy Spirit.

* Morning Star biblical references: Revelation 22:16 "I, Jesus, have sent My angel to testify to you these things in the churches. I am the Root and the Offspring of David, the Bright and Morning Star."

Isaiah 14:12, "How you are fallen from heaven, O Lucifer, son of the morning! How you are cut down to the ground You who weakened the nations!"

Addiction	All drugs, narcotics, pornography, food, sugar, caffeine, social media, movies, relationships, any chemical/emotional dependency on something other than God for fulfillment. Freaks out when deprived of this, withdraws, manipulation of people to get it, manipulation of grace, victim mentality, typically needs a combination of deliverance and time in the Word and possibly a place without the substance option for a while.
Lust	Pornography, looking at women/men, can't get images out of your mind, can't stop thinking about women or men, believes the lie that this is part of your identity, coldness to others, hardness of heart, doesn't want most physical contact, hard time, can't be around a person without having lustful thoughts, perverse thoughts, a gateway to sexual perversions. A hard time of really connecting with people of the opposite gender.
Perversion	All sexual deviations: pedophilia, bestiality, attractions to same gender, sadism, all deviations, fetishes, inordinate affections, sexual violence.
Lying	Can't stop lying, can't tell the truth, exaggerates, blames others, makes yourself look good, exaggerates on stories, tries to control outcome of people's perceptions.
Trauma	Car accidents, all traumatic accidents, sports injuries, all violence done to you, falling, getting hit by a car, getting hit in general, most circumstances that lead to pain or injury, many times people will get healed instantly after trauma spirit is evicted.
Torment	Tormenting thoughts, tormenting actions, fears, nonstop voices in head, tormenting diseases, can't get lies out of your head, thoughts that go on and on in your mind.

Week 9 - Gifts: Sozo

A. Teaching

Sozo

Sozo is a word that describes a process of healing, many times from trauma or from pain. It is very powerful! I know many people who have been saved through an encounter with Jesus because of a sozo they were doing. The word in Greek means to save, heal and deliver.

Here is the reference from Strong's #4982: sozo (pronounced sode'-zo) from a primary sos (contraction for obsolete saos, "safe"); to save, i.e. deliver or protect (literally or figuratively):-- heal, preserve, save (self), do well, be (make) whole.

Sozo sessions are an opportunity to invite the Holy Spirit into your and others' history, remove any drama, and heal any brokenness, past hurt, or hurtful experiences. They are very powerful if done right. You will notice also that the sozo is similar to the deliverance because you are finding the root or lie, and replacing it with a truth and many times with an experience with Jesus, and letting Him lead them into the truth.

A big thing is determining when and where the initial trauma or hurt or pain came in, the first time you remember thinking that thought, or being afraid of people leaving you, or getting angry. Normally, the first time that you remember thinking that thought is where the trauma or demonic influence came in. The way it works is typically this; you are in a traumatic or confusing situation. In the moment you make an agreement with a lie, and from there on out, anytime you get close to that thought or lie, all of a sudden you start to act out. Our goal is to heal that traumatic situation, so it prevents this from happening.

Another very important thing, is to ask Holy Spirit to show where Jesus was in the midst of the trauma. Many, many times, they will get an open vision of Jesus and they will see Him in the mist of the hurt, and He will give them the ability to heal. Remember to always bring it back to identity. We want to make sure that the people are uplifted at the end and reminded of their identity as sons and daughters of God!

The Difference Between Sozo and Deliverance

Deliverance is focusing on removing any demons out of your body causing this pain, hurt, anger, lies etc. In deliverance, we believe that by believing a lie or committing a consistent sin, you are inviting the demonic. So, the goal is to bring truth to the lie, then cast the demon out. Sozo is more focused on the healing and restoration from the same lie or traumatic situation, and bringing the person to an encounter with Jesus. Many times, people will have visions during the sozo and in them Jesus gives truth and life in exchange for the hurt and wounds (lies). There is always an exchange with SOZO. The person gives Jesus the bad stuff, and Jesus gives them the good, transformation stuff!

B. Research, Activation, and Resources

Reading

> **Bible** - At least three chapters a day, beginning in Matthew (meditate on John 4)
>
> **Textbook** – Read the next Week

Watching:

Patricia King - Detoxing Your Mind: An Interview with Dr Caroline Leaf (this is not specific to only sozo)

https://www.youtube.com/watch?v=Ea8pHeetkgo&t=685s

Speaking

Commit to saying 10x a day: "I have the mind of Christ!"

Doing

Sozo Basic Formula

First, ask them (if they don't' know ask Holy Spirit) when did the trauma or hurt pain come in, what was the initial time you remember thinking that thought, or being afraid of people leaving you, or getting angry. "Jesus, what's the root of this problem (fear, rejection, addiction, etc.)?"

Second, ask Holy Spirit to show them where Jesus was in the midst of the trauma, guide them through an encounter with Jesus. Ask questions like "Jesus, what do you want to say to this person about this issue?" What is the lie? What do you want to do with this lie? What's the truth? It's also important to ask the person if they can forgive those who injured them, and lead them in forgiving those who hurt them. Then ask Jesus to close the door to whatever the issue was, and what Jesus would like to give in exchange for this hurt, injury, or lie? If the person says, "it's really hard for me to forgive or I can't forgive", ask them if they would like Jesus to help them to forgive. Wait until they are ready to forgive then proceed. Another good question would be "Jesus, what will happen if they forgive this person?"

Third, always bring it back to identity. We want to make sure that the people are very uplifted at the end and confirmed in their identity as sons and daughters of God!

Week 10 - Gifts: Deliverance on the Street

A. Teaching

I think a huge thing to start off with is our concept of deliverance. Many people think that deliverance is what Hollywood and movies portray it as, such as The Exorcist, or movies about witches or ancient exorcisms.

This is not the case at all. If we look at the first message that Jesus ever publicly preached, it was on deliverance. This was the message He preached to announce who He was and what His ministry was, and if we look closely, we find that it's mostly about deliverance and setting people free. Jesus said, *"the Spirit of the Lord is upon me, because He has anointed me to preach the gospel to the poor; He has sent me to heal the brokenhearted, to proclaim liberty to the captives and recovery of sight to the blind, to set at liberty those who are oppressed"* (Luke 4:18). We see that three out of the five things that He was called to do was setting people free from captivity and emotional hurt, and this is what deliverance is all about. Deliverance is about freedom, about removing the obstacles in people's lives that try and stop them from walking in the abundant life that Jesus promised, and setting them free from the prisons and jails in their minds and bodies.

Many times, we are confused about what deliverance is, and at what point the flesh stops and the demonic starts. Robert Morris, pastor at Gateway Church has a great quote, "You can't disciple a demon, and you can't cast out the flesh". This is a great quote that talks about the difference between demonic oppression and just living out of the flesh. Our flesh has a sin nature, and needs to be renewed through the Word of God and prayer, but if after we have renewed our mind, and we still have an overwhelming desire to live under the slavery of sin, fear, lust and hurt, then there is probably a spirit that needs to be dealt with.

The metaphor that we tell people is, if you are sinking in the ocean, and you have a weight wrapped around your ankle, and we cut the weight off, you will still need to swim or you will drown. But by getting the weight cut off your foot, it makes swimming possible. In other words, casting a demon out of your flesh gives you the <u>ability</u> to successfully transform your mind through the Word and prayer, and actually see consistent freedom in that area. But it <u>does not</u> <u>replace the transformation process of staying in the Word</u>; it just combines with it and makes it possible to live in freedom.

We also see Jesus talk about demons returning. The truth is, every time you invite a demon back into your life through sin, you must cast it out again, or it will try and oppress you. In Matthew 12:43-45, Jesus says, *"When an unclean spirit goes out of a man, he goes through dry places, seeking rest, and finds none. Then he says, 'I will return to my house from which I came.' And when he comes, he finds it empty, swept, and put in order. Then he goes and takes with him seven other spirits more wicked than himself, and they enter and dwell there; and the last state of that man is worse than the first. So shall it also be with this wicked generation."* We tell people it's like having a hotel and inviting people to live in each of your rooms. If you invite a person in your hotel ten times, then each time, you have to invite them out again. Demons will leave, but if you are giving in to a sin consistently, they will start oppressing your flesh. If you get free from that sin and then go back, it will be even harder and there will be more oppression.

When it comes to deliverance on the street, it's good to be bold, and to use wisdom. Many times, the spirits become loud to distract you or to embarrass you, similar to a spoiled child in a store. It's good to not respond, but stay strong in your authority and speak to the spirit, not the person or the response. I also find when doing deliverance on the streets, it's very important to affirm people in their identity, so they understand you're not talking to them, but something that is trying to control them.

From my approach, the easiest thing to do seems to start just praying for them, and then something will pop up. Many times, on the street, through the Holy Spirit, it will be obvious what they are struggling with spiritually. They will ask to get free from the spirit of addiction, they will be angry, or afraid or have rejection (on the streets, confusion or delusion is a big spirit as well). It's very important to rely on the Holy Spirit and ask Him questions if you need to. Don't be embarrassed about doing deliverances in public. Many people are struggling with the demonic and need the freedom to be able to live a good life, which is why deliverance was such a big part of Jesus's ministry.

Don't replace the need for strong biblical teaching and growth with deliverance, but don't replace deliverance with anything; it is a big part of outreach and growth. On a side note, something that helped me, was realizing that it is not possible for a Christian have a demon in their spirit, but just like sickness, demons still try to attack and possess Christians in their flesh. That's why it's important to get them out, so they stop trying to oppress and control our minds, or to attack our bodies.

Many things Jesus paid for, but we need to appropriate with our faith. Similar to salvation, if Jesus dying for our sins was enough to save us, the whole world would be saved. But we have to believe, we have to take a step, we have to move. Deliverance is very similar with Christians; we are already free through Christ, we already have victory, but we need to take this victory with our hands of faith, and push out any lying or deceptive spirits that we have given rights to in the past.

Understanding your authority is very important. If you do not understand your authority, demons will try and scam you into thinking that they are scarier and more powerful than you. It is all an act. When Jesus sent out the seventy early on in His ministry, they could not have been

discipling with Him for very long. Luke 10:7 says, *"Then the seventy returned with joy, saying,*
"Lord, even the demons are subject to us in Your name." All demons must bow at the name of
Jesus.

Ephesians 1 and 2 are very important chapters in the context of your biblical authority. In
Ephesians 1:19-21 states that, *"...what is the exceeding greatness of His power toward us who*
believe, according to the working of His mighty power which He worked in Christ when He raised
Him from the dead and seated Him at His right hand in the heavenly places, far above all
principality and power and might and dominion, and every name that is named, not only in this
age but also in that which is to come." This is amazing, but it doesn't stop there. In Ephesians
2:6 it says, *"and raised us up together, and made us sit together in the heavenly places in Christ*
Jesus." We are seated with Christ above all dominion and power and might! We need to think
of ourselves as seated with Him, and take authority over any lying spirit that would try to hurt
or harm us or others, and SET PEOPLE FREE!

The reason we don't see many successful deliverances is because we don't understand this
authority. When we do, we don't practice enough or persevere during a deliverance. If we were
to practice more, we would see more. I've now seen hundreds of deliverances and much
freedom through it: people going off medications, schizophrenic spirits with voices leaving,
bipolar with chemical imbalances being healed, anger leaving, depression leaving, people who
have slept with the lights on their whole life get completely free from terror so turn the lights
off. In that last example is a very interesting story - this girl came into one of our workshops,
she was in hear late twenties and she had never slept with the light out and struggled with
deep fears and terrors. We prayed for her a couple times without much release or change; then
after I asked, she started telling me she also had sleep paralysis and would wake up with in
terror. I was filled with so much anger; right then, the Holy Spirit highlighted spirits of terror
and torment. We commanded with deep passion to see her free and then kicked the spirits out.
She screamed, then she got filled with joy and the Holy Spirit. I followed up with her
roommates a few months later who confirmed that now she sleeps like a log with the lights out
and no fear.

Many things have a spiritual origin and a natural manifestation, so we mistakenly try and treat the manifestation, instead of trying to heal the origin. If you go for the manifestation instead of the root, it will always grow back.

I would encourage you guys to not give up, but keep pressing through. Many times, on the streets especially with homeless, there's a spirit of delusion and confusion on their mind. 2 Corinthians 4:4 says, "whose minds the god of this age has blinded, who do not believe, lest the light of the gospel of the glory of Christ, who is the image of God, should shine on them." If you can just pray for them, and put your hands on their head, and let the Holy Spirit's peace flood their minds, normally you can get much further with the deliverance after that. Always pray with your eyes open if possible.

B. Research, Activation, and Resources

Reading

>**Bible** - At least three chapters a day, beginning in Matthew (meditate on deliverance of legion)

>**Textbook** - Read the next Week

>**Required Reading:** Pigs in the Parlor, Frank Hammond

>**Suggested Reading:** Biblical Foundations of Freedom, Art Mathias

Watching:

>Art Montgomery - JEZEBEL STRIKES AGAIN

>https://www.youtube.com/watch?v=Je4JUIg42K8&list=PLhDKyqhmoOJztM4in5zvubOcS9TtWCPME

>Art Montgomery -DEMONS COME OUT OF THIS BACKSLIDDEN CHRISTIAN.

>https://www.youtube.com/watch?v=-1Ob1-lMQJQ

>Art Montgomery - DELIVERANCE FROM THE DEMON OF CRYSTAL METH ON THE STREET

>https://www.youtube.com/watch?v=sgxwrGoK9r4

Speaking

Commit to saying ten times a day: "I am seated with Christ above all powers, and dominions and authorities!"

Doing

Perform one to three deliverances on the street with you leading, and be involved in two others this next week.

Decide in your heart to shift your perspective of spirits from one of fear or hesitation to one of power and authority. Decide to think of deliverance as not a crazy manifestation or weird exorcisms but going into dark places and setting sons and daughters free from prison.

a. **Where is there a loss of control, sin or oppression, when did it start?** (Romans 6:16). Each time you invite a demon back through sin or believing a lie, you must kick it out again (Luke 11:25).

Example: If it's a fear, "when do you first remember feeling afraid?"

b. **Have them REPENT and turn away from any sin involved and denounce the lie they believed and break agreement.**

Example: "I'm sorry for not believing God would protect me; and in Jesus name I denounce a spirit of fear."

c. **Cast the demon out with authority!** (Matthew 10:1, Matthew 8:16)

Example: "In Jesus name, I command you demon to leave them."

d. **If the demon is lingering, command more (Holy Spirit) Fire on that area of their body!**

e. **Repeat till you feel release or get a word.**

f. **Affirm them in their identity as sons and daughters of God and ask God to bless their lives!**

Passing

Assignments are due at the beginning of the following class.

☐ Have you had an opportunity to believe for your healing this week? Have you received the revelation of God's heart for you to be 100% healed yet? Please Explain _____

_____

_____

☐ Have you read the next Week in your workbook?

☐ Have you read and finished Christ the Healer?

Week 11 - Gifts: Prophecy

A. Teaching

Prophecy is considered by Paul to be the most important gift that should be pursued; at least inside of the church. He says above all, wish that you might prophecy (1 Corinthians 14:5). Prophesy is incredibly important because it is one of the main gifts that shows God's direct love for people, and His concern with the details of their lives and futures. All the gifts are God's way of saying, "I am real, I am your Father and I love you." People getting healed shows God's compassion in their bodies; deliverance shows God's compassion in setting them free. But with prophecy, it is God directly speaking His truth over their lives. This will cancel all the lies, hurt, pain, and disappointment that they have experienced throughout their life. Prophecy is a direct funnel of God's love to people's hearts, and a very important work of the Holy Spirit.

There are many examples of prophecy in the Bible. When Jesus is talking to Peter and says, *"Peter on this rock I will build my church and the gates of hell will not prevail against it"* (Matthew 16:18), that was a version of prophecy. Jesus is speaking the truth of God over Peter's life and Peter's future.

2 Corinthians 1:3-5 says that prophecy is for encouragement, exhortation, and edification. Typically, we see prophecy as a gift used to build people up in their identities and future. It is a very important gift and needs to be pushed to the top.

Two Practical Steps to Walk in Prophecy

Step 1 options:

- ☐ Close your eyes and ask the Holy Spirit to show you about the person.

- ☐ Ask God to show you how he sees that person, and then just start describing God's description to them.

- ☐ Start encouraging them, and speaking truth over them, and after a while, let the Holy Spirit take over. Many times, just starting with encouragement in faith will end in prophecy.

- ☐ Often, the Holy Spirit will show you a word or a picture to get you started. As you take a step of faith and speak out the word or the picture, just like unwinding a ball of string, you will start to get more revelation. The key is taking the initial step of faith.

Step 2

Describe what you see to the person, do it in faith, and trust God to finish the sentence. Psalm 81:10 says, *"open your mouth wide and I will fill it."* Luke 12:11 also says, *"When you stand before kings and priests don't think what you're going to say, behold my spirit will speak through you."*

As with most of the gifts, faith plays a huge part, as does learning how to act in expectancy before we see God show up. The cool thing about prophecy and words of knowledge is, they also teach us to start distinguishing the voice and the communication of the Holy Spirit, which in life, ministry and evangelism is indispensable!

Prophecy is giving your mouth the ability to speak the Word of God through you to that person. The most important thing is just taking that step, and starting to describe what you see, what you hear or what you feel about them, and letting the Holy Spirit take over.

Remember much prophecy starts with a step of faith and believing that God is actually giving you a word. As you start your word, keep going and finish it. Do not be surprised if the majority of the prophecy is encouraging; most prophecy is for encouragement.

That being said, something negative could be from God. Remember the women at the well. Jesus's Word of prophecy that she was on her fifth marriage and affair, would not be considered by most to be edifying, encouraging, or exhorting, but the woman was saved, and so was the whole village (John 4:1-42). This being said, most of prophecy will be more positive and encouraging according to Corinthians 14. Sometimes life is hard for people, and a strong word of prophecy will cause a shift in their whole atmosphere, attitude, and life.

I would encourage you, especially initially, to be wise about specifics, and be wise about directive words of prophecy. In other words, telling people to do things, go places, marry people. You want to make sure you can very clearly hear God, before you step out into these areas. Sometimes people's lives have been hurt listening too much to prophesy and acting on words, instead of taking it home and listening to the Holy Spirit. Prophecy is not a replacement for the Holy Spirit, it is merely a tool He uses to touch people inside and outside of the church.

B. Research, Activation, and Resources

Reading

> **Bible** - At least three chapters a day, beginning in Matthew (meditate on John 4)
>
> **Textbook** – Read the next Week

Watching

> Patricia King - Activating Your Prophetic Gift
>
> https://www.youtube.com/watch?v=Vn5TK_3e7vk
>
> Jason Chin - HOW TO PROPHESY
>
> https://www.youtube.com/watch?v=hs7xOXytBuM

Speaking

> Each day for the next 10 days, commit to prophesying over yourself and speaking God's truth and life over 3 things - your health, your finances and your relationships!

Doing

- Give prophecies to at least three people in a church/workshop setting, give three prophecies on the street this week.
- Schedule and go through a sozo in the next two weeks.

Prophecy Basic Formula

First, the first step is close your eyes and ask Holy Spirit to show you about the person, another good way to start, would be just asking God to show you how he sees that person and then just start describing this to them.

Second, the second step is to take a step of boldness and faith and describe what you see in the person, do it in faith, and trust Holy Spirit to give you the words once you have started, and He will! Also, pay attention to your feelings, because God may give you emotional revelation for this person.

Passing

Assignments are due at the beginning of the following class.

Have you:

☐ Performed perform one to three deliverances on yourself?

☐ Gone through the Deliverance Inventory above and seen if you identify with a major loss of control, sin or hurt in any of those areas? Please explain

_____

_____

_____

_____

_____

_____

☐ Read the next Week in your workbook?

☐ Watched the three Art deliverance videos?

☐ Chosen to set aside time this week for quiet time and reading and praying? Please expound _____

_____

Week 12 - Gifts: Word of Knowledge/Wisdom

A. Teaching

The word of knowledge is a very important gift of the Spirit. Giving the word of knowledge is the ability to tell someone something about their life, that there is no way you can know. This has such a strong evangelical power. Think about this - at the Samaritan well, no dead person was raised, no leper was cleansed, not even a blind person was healed. When Jesus was with the woman at the well, He just gave her one word of knowledge in His prophecy to her, and the whole village came back and believed in him (John 4). One word of knowledge spoken at the right time and in the right way will have such a strong evangelical impact.

It's very important to learn how to operate in the gift of word of knowledge. Like most of the gifts, this should be earnestly desired. Paul says to earnestly desire of the best gifts (1 Corinthians 12:31). Word of knowledge is definitely one of the better gifts. If you operate in this correctly, people will be confused and maybe even think you of have some type of superpower. Just remember what Daniel said about his ability to interpret dreams - that all this power comes from God.

To practice the word of knowledge, it's very similar to prophesy. All you have to do is say: "Holy Spirit show me something about this person, that only You could know." Many times, you'll see a picture, a word, or get an impression and it will be right on. The first time I taught on word of knowledge, I had actually never practiced it before, I have just been praying for people, and God would show me hidden things about them or their lives. It would come out while I was praying for them, but I had not just been practicing doing it off the cuff, without being in a prayer flow (the more time you spend in secret place prayer, the easier the gifts become). I was a little bit uncertain if it would work that way, but the Holy Spirit is so faithful. We split up into groups of three people, and God gave me one or two words for each person, and they were all right on; the people were astounded.

A good way to practice this is to say, "Holy Spirit show me a vision image or word about someone." Then take that step of faith and start speaking it out, and don't stop until you feel peace to stop. Normally, the first few sentences are just the opening; He will give you more words when you start out in faith.

A word of wisdom is like a word of knowledge, except a word of knowledge is information about a person. A word of wisdom is typically a specific direction they should go or something they should do, or a solution to a problem, many times with practical steps.

Remember, a word of knowledge and word of wisdom normally go hand-in-hand. We see these two gifts working with Joseph in Genesis. While he is interpreting Pharaoh's dream, he has divine insight into the famine problem. Then he has a divine solution to the problem, to store up more grain. Notice that Joseph had supernatural insight to the problem. The solution however, involved Pharaoh doing something (Genesis 41). Word of wisdom is much more directive and many times involves action. It's very important to listen to the Holy Spirit on this if you're telling someone something that you feel they should do. I encourage people to take what I give them home and pray about it, and make sure that the Holy Spirit living inside of them confirms this word. When I have people confirm with the Holy Spirit a word I give them, then I am not telling them something they need to do with their lives. This removes the possibility of mis-instructing them or being guilty of control issues.

Activating the word of wisdom also requires a step of faith, and giving a word of wisdom to someone needs to be acted out in faith and expectancy. James 1:5 says, *"if any man lacks wisdom, let him ask of God who gives to all men liberally."* Word of wisdom many times will come right after a word of knowledge, especially if there is something they need to do to see the breakthrough they may be seeking. Another good way to activate the word of wisdom is if someone has a problem, ask the Holy Spirit right then for a divine solution to their problem, and to show you both wisdom and knowledge, and then describe what He shows you. Yesterday morning at our Church service Brooke, one of the new girls in our class, ran up to me and said: "It's working!" She said, "since our outreach last Friday, I have been getting non-stop words for people, this is incredible!"

One of the important parts of the word of wisdom is, this gets each of us involved with hearing God's voice about our specific problems, and with trusting His solutions. And believe me, they work very well. Learning to hear the Holy Spirit's voice is one of the most important aspects of doing anything in the supernatural; this needs to be treasured and sought after in prayer. Moving in all of these gifts, we are really learning to move in a partnership (we call it a partnership, but He leads the partnership) with the Holy Spirit and God's will for our lives!

B. Research, Activation, and Resources

Reading

    Bible - At least three chapters a day, beginning in Matthew (meditate on Genesis 37).

    Textbook – Read the next Week

Watching:

    Jason Chin - Word of Knowledge Basics

    https://www.youtube.com/watch?v=g94DMZvujCM

    Kenneth E Hagin - The Revelation Gifts 03 - Word of Wisdom

    https://www.youtube.com/watch?v=tuinFKftecc

Church Tsidkenu - Girl Gets Wrecked with God's Love at 85 Degrees!

https://www.youtube.com/watch?v=Xn4KUdL8qBU

Doing

Give at least three words of knowledge this week, at least one in the class and one on the street. Give one word of wisdom this week.

1. Consider the importance of moving in the word of wisdom and knowledge and practice hearing Holy Spirit's voice by asking specific questions and then acting them out when you hear the answers.

2. Ask the Holy Spirit for a word of knowledge or wisdom for someone.

3. Find someone to practice with.

   a. Ask them about a problem or difficult situation in their life, whether great or small.

   b. Ask the Holy Spirit for a word of wisdom for them and that situation.

   c. Step out and practice the word.

   d. Ask the Holy Spirit for a word of knowledge for them.

   e. You will see a picture, a word, an impression, something.

   f. Step out in faith and tell them what you see, no matter how small or silly it seems. I have personally seen random people completely wrecked over words like: "pumpkin" "blackbird" and "peanut butter and jelly".

Passing

Assignments are due at the beginning of the following class.

☐ Have you given prophecies to at least three people in a church or workshop setting?

☐ Have you given three prophecies on the street this week?

☐ Have you scheduled and/or gone through a sozo in the next two weeks?

   ○ Please explain_____

☐ Have you read the next Week in your workbook?

☐ Have you watched the three prophecy YouTube videos?

☐ Have you chosen to set aside time this week for quiet time and reading and praying?

   Please expound_____

Week 13 - Baptize in the Holy Spirit and Fiyah

A. Teaching

This is one of my favorite things to do in evangelism. I love praying for people to get filled with the Holy Spirit and fire!

Here is a quick story on how powerful it can be just getting people to feel the presence of God. We were in a Muslim refugee camp outside of Dunkirk, France. And before we went, everyone told us we could not talk about Jesus at all. They said if we use the name of Jesus, people would at least get offended, and at the worst get violent. In this Muslim refugee camp, once you get in, there are no police. You are just by yourself, surrounded by many refugees. When we went there, all of the women and children were hidden in the woods, so there were just a few hundred young Muslim men.

We started doing what they said not to do; we spoke about Jesus because we are a little hard headed, ha-ha. Initially most of them rejected Him and some started to get angry. Right then we decided to just do what we're good at doing, and what we have been doing on the streets in

San Diego for years now. We asked them if they wanted to feel the Holy Spirit, or if they had pain in their body. Many were from Pakistan, and Iraq and spoke only some English. They asked what name we would be praying in, and we said we just pray for a touch from Holy Spirit. They said, "Holy Spirit is fine", not a single one turned us down. We prayed for them. After a few minutes, they all started to feel the presence of God and started shaking, laughing, and becoming full of joy. After thirty minutes, I had a line of five Muslim men who I start praying over, and they started falling out in the Spirit. It was one of the craziest experiences of my life. At first remember, they were so resistant to Jesus and even threatening, but after they started experiencing the Holy Spirit's presence and healing and deliverance power, they got so hungry and excited! Psalms 34:8 says "*taste and see that the Lord is good*", after they "tasted" His presence and healings they asked "What is that?" We then said "that's Jesus!" and they all wanted Him! We had many grab our hands one by one and lead us away from the rest of the crowds and tell us "It's not safe for me to say this over there, but I want to know your Jesus!" So much fruit; we all got wrecked. By the end of the two days, we had led about sixty Muslims to Jesus. Jesus said, "*the Comforter, which is the Holy Ghost, whom the Father will send in my name, he shall teach you all things, and bring all things to your remembrance, whatsoever I have said unto you*" (John 14:26). We found this to be very true.

Many times, people are hesitant to follow Jesus even in America, and I ask if I can pray for them to feel the presence of God, the Holy Spirit overwhelms them, and they want all of Jesus! The trick with this is knowing how to get people to have an encounter with God through healing, deliverance or feeling His presence then they want Him. Romans 2:4 says, "*..knowing that the goodness of God leadeth thee to repentance...*". Psalms 16:11 also says "*in your presence is fullness of joy.*" My goal is to get to experience the fullness of joy, the goodness of God through His Holy Spirit, and that WILL lead many of them to repentance, even if they don't have any pain in their body, or any visible demons.

Another good question is, how important is getting them to speak right away with the gift of tongues? I would say the gift of tongues is one of the most important manifestations of the Holy Spirit. Paul says in 1 Corinthians 14:18, "*I thank God that I speak in tongues more than all of you*" and then he says in verse 39, "*...and do not forbid speaking in tongues*". Many people think that tongues are a special gift only for some, and some people have it and some people don't; but Mark 16:17-18 says *"and these signs shall follow them that believe; In my name shall they cast out devils; they shall speak with new tongues."* Tongues are for the believers, not just the gifted). Furthermore, Paul says, not everyone operates in all the gifts. But his solution to this problem is not to say "that's not my gift" but to *"eagerly desire the greater gifts"* (1 Corinthians 12:31.) So even if you think tongues is only a gift that some people have, it's one of the better ones, and it's time to earnestly desire it!

I have so many stories with tongues, it's crazy. I have decided in my life and in my heart to pray for one to two hours every day, and almost all of that is in the Spirit, every once a while I'll have something that I pray for in English, but most of my prayers are in tongues, and they make a huge, huge difference!

Many times, things come up and I don't know what to do in a deliverance, so I will start praying in tongues. I remember one time, we were doing a deliverance with a woman who had been caught up in witchcraft for a long time, and she considered herself a very powerful witch. We did a deliverance on her. There was a lot of stuff that came with freedom, and we felt super strongly that God wanted her to speak in tongues. But she would not give in to the loss of control, and sure enough, a few months later she was back close to where she started.

Tongues is a heavenly language and is literally the voice of the Holy Spirit when we pray in tongues. The Holy Spirit is prophesying good things over us and interceding for us, as it says in Romans 8:26, *"For we know not what we should pray for as we ought: but the Spirit itself makes intercession for us with groanings which cannot be uttered."* We don't know how to pray, so we need Holy Spirit to pray for our weakness, so we don't have weakness, and can do the will of God perfectly! There are many things that need to be prayed out that the only way to do it is by the gift of tongues. 1 Corinthians 14:2 says, *"For he who speaks in a tongue does not speak to men but to God, for no one understands him; however, in the Spirit he speaks mysteries."* I have also found that when praying for people to receive the Holy Spirit and activate their tongues, praying over them in tongues really helps!

Teach people that we are to have a relationship with Holy Spirit. We are to ask Him if we don't understand anything in the Word or about life, as well as asking pastors, but the Holy Spirit is always the most personnel since He lives in you. 1 John 2:27 says, *"But the anointing which you have received from Him abides in you, and you do not need that anyone teach you; but as the same anointing teaches you concerning all things, and is true, and is not a lie, and just as it has taught you, you will abide in Him."* Also, we need to get filled daily with Holy Spirit through worship, singing, and praying in tongues!

A prayer for boldness

In Acts 4:23-31 there is a very good prayer the disciples pray for boldness and miracles in the context of evangelism, *"Now, Lord, look on their threats, and grant to Your servants that with all boldness they may speak Your Word, by stretching out Your hand to heal, and that signs and wonders may be done through the name of Your holy Servant Jesus."* ... *"And when they had prayed, the place where they were assembled together was shaken; and they were all filled with the Holy Spirit, and they spoke the Word of God with boldness."* The crazy thing about this prayer is that all the disciples were already filled with the Holy Spirit and so this was a second filling and an empowerment to be bold and work miracles of God!

Remember guys, baptizing people in Holy Spirit and Fire is so, so important, many people in our Church and personal long-time friends of mine have not been able to kick their addictions till they get FILLED with the Holy Spirit and Fire! I was at a young people's service in LA area and this girl showed up, and I knew from the Holy Spirit that she had some major issues, she wore dark sunglasses, but looked very normal for the most part. I started praying for her with a good friend Earl, and giving her words of knowledge. It turned out she was on heroin right then and had major depression and suicidal thoughts. We prayed for her and it broke off. By the end of the night, she got instantly sobered, delivered from the addiction spirit, filled Holy Spirit and speaking in other tongues. I wish you could have seen her, she was so joyful and light by then.

My good friend Art was out praying for people 6 months ago and he and Michael Tucker encountered a drug dealer. They asked if they could pray for him. They did, and he fell out in the street in the Holy Spirit and was out for a while. When he came back up, he was a different person. He said that his mom always used to tell him about this baptism of the Holy Spirit, but he never believed it! He was so wrecked in the Holy Spirit. We tell all the sons and daughters getting set free from addictions that there is no high like the Most High!

We go to Mexico all the time and each time we see 20 or so people baptized in the Holy Spirit and speaking with other tongues. Many of them are high when they start speaking, and 10 minutes later sober when they finish. We have seen prostitutes and hit men from cartels get filled with Holy Spirit and Fire and fall out in the streets in America and Tijuana, and get up ready for Jesus. When we do follow up, many of them are still just as transformed - come on Jesus!

Art says "Ben, with the Holy Spirit, overdo it", so that's what we do; and when we do it, more people always hear and give their lives to Jesus; ha-ha!

A last story for this Week and one of the cooler ones, I was out praying for people downtown last Thursday. One of the security guards ran up to me. (We had prayed for him two weeks ago and now He comes to Church and is a wrecked Jesus lover.) He said a man was lying on the street screaming that he was going to kill himself and others! He said, "I know you guys move in the power of God, please do something!" I ran over with Mark Debois, and he was lying in the middle of the street with a cone around him. The security guards were about 25 feet away just watching. I asked if I could pray for him. After a bit, he said yes; as Mark and I prayed for him, the Holy Spirit dropped on the situation and peace came over him instantly. He let me put my hand on his forehead and I knew it was over! He was standing up. The presence of God had hit him so hard, he fell out on the street and came up a different person! He said he wanted to murder two people and knew now that it was wrong. I led him into a prayer, he forgave them, and received Jesus and the Holy Spirit; what an amazing night!

Guys we hear stories like this from people in our schools and Church all the time, I literally get texts every day talking about God's power and transformation! Never underestimate the Power of the baptism in the Holy Spirit and the difference that will make for you and everyone you pray for! Most of the people in our Church are very active in that, sometimes it happens quickly, sometimes slowly, but it always happens:)! Now let's grow in it!

B. Research, Activation, and Resources

Reading

Bible - At least three chapters a day, beginning in Matthew (meditate on Acts 19:1-6).

Textbook – next Week

Watching

Church Tsidkenu - "DEATH OUT, HOLY SPIRIT IN!!"

https://www.youtube.com/watch?v=Xkb12W5rmhw&t=43s

Church Tsidkenu - "San Diego United Tent Revival"

https://www.youtube.com/watch?v=oZXBxxFvAfY

Doing

Choose to baptize one to three people this week in Holy Spirit and Fire and at least one with new tongues. If possible, do one in the workshop and one on the street.

1.   Be expectant (Mark 11:24).

2.   Teach them not to be afraid of the Holy Spirit, but to start expecting to receive Him because God is a good Father and will gives them GOOD gifts ONLY (Luke 11:13).

3.   Have someone stand behind them as an act of faith in case they fall, tell them that as well. (2nd Chron 5:14).

4.   Have them say, "Jesus baptize me with your Holy Spirit baptize and fire and the gift of tongues" or "Jesus I'm precious to you, baptize me with your Holy Spirit and Tongues".

5.   Ask the Holy Spirit to fill them, and put your hand on their heart, belly or forehead (ask permission first) and pray (in tongues out loud) until you sense they are filled with the Holy Spirit. If they don't' speak in tongues right away, coach them in it, sometimes having them imitate your tongues to break through the mind-spirit disconnect (Acts 8:18) (John 7:38).

6.   Listen to the Holy Spirit! (Romans 8:14).

Decide in your heart, to shift your Holy Spirit perspective from fearing to engage with Him, to recognizing that He is your major Helper and Comforter!

Passing

Assignments are due at the beginning of the following class.

☐ Have you found people with mortal conditions, people who are blind, mute, to pray for? People without limbs? People who are dying? Were you persistent and expected a breakthrough? Please explain.

_____

_____

_____

_____

_____

_____

_____

_____

_____

☐ Have you read the next Week in your workbook?

☐ Have you fully read They Told Me Their Stories by Tommy Welchel?

☐ Have you chosen to set aside time this week for quiet time and reading and praying? Please expound.

_____

_____

_____

_____

_____

_____

_____

A. Teaching

One of the biggest tips that I've learned about moving in the supernatural is to stop using my natural mind. Please don't misunderstand me. I still renew my mind to the Word of God and stay in the Word of God. But sometimes in the midst of believing for a huge miracle, or persisting for a miracle, I find my natural brain to be of no use. In fact, it is getting in the way, telling me that "they won't get healed", or "to get out of that situation ASAP", or freaking out! Many times, I feel a type of fight or flight mode kicking in. I need to be at peace and focus on the healing at hand. I have learned to turn my brain off.

Romans 8:7 says, *"the carnal mind is enmity against God: for it is not subject to the law of God, neither indeed can be."* Therefore, sometimes the carnal mind just needs to be turned off. The easiest way to do this is to stop thinking about anything in your head, and push all your thoughts out, like you were meditating on nothing. The Holy Spirit does not live inside of your head; He lives with your spirit (remember, this is more towards your stomach region). I like to drop out of my mind and drop in my spirit, and do my thinking with my spirit, not my head.

Remember, Ephesians 4:23 says to *"be renewed in the spirit of your mind"*; we have a spiritual mind, not just a natural mind. I like my mind to be completely empty so that the Holy Spirit flows through me. If I micromanage the Holy Spirit with my thought process, I can leave the situation before the situation is finished and before the person is set free, lead or filled.

Your Approach

Jesus compares winning souls to fishing, therefore just like with fishing, we need to use wisdom when learning how to do it, so it's the most effective to catch the most fish. On that note, Proverbs 11:30 says that he/she who wins souls is wise. And Jesus says in the context of evangelism, to be *"wise as serpents and harmless as doves"* (Matthew 10:16).

I have a couple of approaches I like, but I would encourage everyone to find the best one for you. The goal of an approach is to create some interpersonal trust and build value in your gospel proposal. I say, "Hi my name is Ben Wisan, my friends and I go all over San Diego loving and praying for people. We have seen hundreds of healings for knees, cancer, and backs. I saw you over here with your cane and I was like, 'I wonder if he would let me pray for him? Do you have any pain in your body?' Or, 'Hi, my friends and I are going around loving on people and practicing praying for people, would you mind if we practiced with you?' In Spanish we ask: "Tiene dolor en su cuerpo?" and if they say "si, porque?" we say "porqué oración y no más dolor." And then we pray for them and Jesus heals them. Your language doesn't have to be perfect if you're moving in the power of God.

Expectancy

Expectancy, we've touched on this a little bit, but expectancy is really the key to most miracles. We need to expect in our hearts for God to show up. The Bible says in Romans 10, "with the heart man believeth unto righteousness, and with the mouth, confession is made unto salvation". Jesus says in Mark 11:23 that *"...if we do not doubt in our hearts..."* (Mark 11:23). It's very important to understand that faith is from the heart/spirit, not the mind. We renew our minds in the Word so that the revelation can drop from our minds to our spirit. <u>If we can get in touch with just keeping our brains off and choosing to believe from our spirit when we are praying for healings and miracles, it will change everything.</u>

We need to learn how to expect someone to be healed and see them healed from our spirit, not our mind, while we're praying for them. We will see many more miracles. It's pretty awesome; I've seen deaf ears open up with this, mute people speak, hernias dissolve and hundreds of knees and backs healed. For everyone I pray in Jesus name, the pain leaves or goes down.

Choose to always be expectant! Remember, Jesus said, according to your faith be it done unto you. Your expectancy needs to always be set before you go into praying for someone that 100% of the time, 100% of the people, get 100% healed, the first time.

TIP: Never rationalize why people don't get healed

If you see someone not get healed, or feel doubt trying to creep in, never ever side with it, or try and figure it out. I have had thoughts of doubt in the past, then tried to rationalize why someone didn't get healed. When I first started, I would side with it, and try to explain away why they didn't get healed. Now I choose to not worry about it, and fully expect the next person to get 100% healed. These temptations to rationalize are almost always just before I see huge, crazy awesome miracles breakout!

One time we were in Ensenada Mexico when we first started praying for healings, and we were praying for this guy's leg, but we couldn't seem to get it to grow out no matter how much we prayed. We left a little bit frustrated because it didn't' grow out (now we know it was most likely just a spirit) and as we continued on our day, we started to rationalize and say things like 'maybe it didn't work because of this' 'maybe he didn't have enough faith' 'maybe it was witchcraft' 'maybe we didn't read our bible enough'.   Right away the Holy Spirit convicted me and said very strongly, "Ben don't rationalize it, only believe!". After I heard that, I said "I don't know why he didn't get healed, but I do know that my expectancy moving forward is: 100% of the time, 100% of the people will get 100% healed, the first time." Later in the day, as we started going through Ensenada, almost everyone we prayed for received instant healing and many believed on Jesus; that day many in the town got wrecked!

Practice, Practice, Practice

One of the most important tips is to practice, practice, practice.

One time almost three years ago, I was leading a Bible study with some guys I was discipling and we were asking ourselves why we don't see the miraculous too much? Or why when we pray for people, we don't see them hardly ever get healed like what happens in the bible. The Holy Spirit is so faithful; He gave me a revelation on the spot - the reason we don't see it is because we are not in practice.

If you got up to give a public speech and had not prepared anything you would start to freak out when it was time to give the speech. If you got up to play a football game and had not been in practice, you would not know what to do or how to do it and may freak out during your first game. It's the same thing with healing for people. We are supposed to be out praying for people, healing people, delivering people, and bringing the kingdom of God to Earth (Mark 16:17-18).

Since we are not out practicing, when a relative or friend gets sick or someone in the church, we immediately try and muster up faith and expectancy that we haven't used in years, and hope that it works. Many times, it doesn't because we have not been practicing on the lost; when it doesn't work because we are not practicing, we blame ourselves or God.

I never thought it would come naturally to me, but I can honestly say now every time I pray for people, I expect them to get healed. I am very comfortable praying for people. God always shows up and I always keep my brain off. But we need to practice it, until it becomes second nature to pray for someone while expecting a miracle.

TIP: Ask Permission, Record Testimonies and LET'S MAKE JESUS FAMOUS.

Okay, one of the biggest tools we have to preach the gospel of Jesus Christ around the world is technology. They did not have this back in the Bible days and this a huge asset for changing the world with God's power. Some people think that posting testimonies is not biblical, because it can bring personal glory, or because they feel you aren't supposed to talk about the good things you do. Let me quickly settle those things on a biblical basis. First, we always need to give God glory when talking about testimonies. Testimonies are never ever to bring personal fame, but to advance the kingdom of Jesus Christ. When you post testimonies, make sure to say something like "Look what Jesus did", "Glory to God who healed this man", etc. Don't be weird about it; God looks at your heart, but give honor to God.

The disciples were very careful to never take glory for what God did (Acts 3:16) (Acts 14:12-14). He uses you because you're yielded, but <u>He is the one who is working power through you.</u> Second, when the bible says keep what you do hidden and *"not let your right hand know what your left is doing"* it's talking about giving money to the poor, not giving testimony of God's miracles (Matthew 6:3). What's the difference? Telling people about what you gave, will bring glory to you because it's your money. Telling people what God did, will bring Him glory, because it's His power. This will create a consumable platform to preach the Good News Message!

Did Jesus Say Not to Talk About Miracles?

The only reason Jesus told people to not talk about the miracles He was doing, was because of the timing of Heaven. He knew people would try and take Him by force to be their earthly king, and that wasn't His destiny.

We see this in John 6:14-15, *"Then those men,* **when they had seen the sign** *that Jesus did, said, "This is truly the Prophet who is to come into the world."* Therefore, when Jesus perceived that they were about to come and take Him by force to make Him king, He departed again to the mountain by Himself alone."

Tell How Much God Has Done

Jesus said, *"let your light shine before others, so that they may see your good works and give glory to your Father who is in heaven"* (Matthew 5:17). We are supposed to preach the gospel of the kingdom, and one of the best ways to do this is through testimonies, so people will glorify God. We see this in Matthew 9:6-8 where Jesus heals a paralyzed man, and the people glorify God. *"But when the multitudes saw it, they marveled and glorified God, which had given such power unto men."* We see Jesus instructing that man to tell of the miracles God has done for him. Again, Jesus casts out a demon and tells the man to *"Return to your own house, and tell what great things God has done for you." And he went his way and proclaimed throughout the whole city what great things Jesus had done for him."* (Luke 8:39).

The Request

To request if you can record a healing shouldn't be weird at all. It's all how you approach it. We just like to say things like "can I get a video of you for teaching others how to do miracles?" and normally people will say "yes." Just remember since you're walking in love, and also for legal reasons, it is very important to always ask for permission before recording people.

The Camera

I would recommend getting a little small camera like a GoPro. We use the Akaso EK7000 and it works great; and is typically cheaper than the bigger name brands. You can also use your phone camera if it's easier.

Social Media

Post your testimonies on social media, **give God all the glory in the post** and let's build America's faith in the God of Miracles again! There is enough garbage all over social media, so let's flood the waves with miracles of the goodness of God. Just remember, and this is very important, to not steal God's glory. You are not doing this to become popular with more people or to promote your own agenda, but to preach the Gospel of Jesus to a generation that needs to see Him! *"If I had not done among them the miracles which none other man did, they had not had sin: but now have they both seen..."* (John 15:24)

Evangelism is like Fishing

Do you realize that evangelism is like fishing? Jesus said to the disciples who are actually fisherman *"come follow after Me, and I will make you fishers of men"* (Matthew 4:19). We need to realize that evangelism is very similar to fishing; otherwise, it's easy to get frustrated and give up early. With fishing, we throw the line in ten times, and maybe one out of ten times you pull up a fish. Sometimes you have a fishing hole where they're all biting and you pull in a bunch at once, and sometimes it seems like you're not catching anything. The trick is persistence, practice, and proper teaching, and then you will start pulling up fish all the time. Jesus would not need to teach the disciples how to fish for people if it wasn't a skill you had to acquire over time.

I have talked to many people who were a day or an hour away from committing suicide. Many people have been begging God all day for a word from Him. You will be the answer to their problem if you go and do not give up. Think of it like fishing for literal fish. It takes patience and perseverance. Many times, you have to throw your line in the water ten times to get a bite, but when you do get one it is one of the most exciting moments of your life. You reel them in, take a picture, lie about the size (kidding), and put the picture on your wall. Remember, Jesus says that we are fishers of men, and will have to <u>have patience and perseverance</u> to keep throwing your line in and to keep asking people if you can pray for them, but as you start to see people get saved and healed, it's the most exhilarating feeling you have ever felt. You just know you are in God's perfect will in those moments!

Rejection

Not every person you talk to you is going to want to get healed. Some people may not want to talk to you. Some people will want nothing to do with you. Jesus promised persecution from some, as well as ready acceptance from others. Some people will be waiting, praying, and hoping you are the answer to their problem.

I have talked to many people who were a day or an hour away from committing suicide. Many people have been begging God all day for a word from Him. You will be the answer to their problem if you go and not give up.

B. Research, Activation, and Resources

Reading

> **Bible** - At least three chapters a day, beginning in Matthew (meditate on Mark 6).
>
> **Textbook** – next Week
>
> **Suggested Reading:** The Miracle of the Scarlet Thread, John Booker

Watching

> Church Tsidkenu - DEAF GIRL HEALED!
>
> https://www.youtube.com/watch?v=Hh72fMRE5qM&t=22s
>
> Art Montgomery - HOW TO GET BOLDNESS IN 5 MINUTES TO DEMONSTRATE MIRACLES
>
> https://www.youtube.com/watch?v=08QXvlLVWqY&t=10s

Speaking

> Commit to saying ten times a day: "100% of the time, 100% of the people get 100% healed the first time."

Doing

> Decide **in your heart to shift your belief system to this:**
>
> 1. Practice Turning your brain off.
> 2. Choose to not rationalize why people don't' get healed.

Passing

Assignments are due at the beginning of the following class.

☐ Have you lead one to three people to Jesus this past week? Please explain.

_____

_____

_____

_____

_____

_____

_____

☐ Have you read the next Week in your workbook?

☐ Have you watched "HOW TO GET BOLDNESS IN 5 MINUTES TO DEMONSTRATE MIRACLES" every day?

☐ Have you chosen to set aside time this week for quiet time and reading and praying? Please expound.

_____

_____

_____

_____

_____

_____

_____

A. Teaching

One misconception is that a Christian NEEDS their own faith to get healed. Many times, we believe that Christians don't get healed because they don't have their own faith. In other words, if I pray for Jane who is a Christian, but she is not in faith, even though I am, that she will not get healed.

I want to talk about this because this can get in the way of your expectancy for people to get healed. One of the main passages used to support this misconception is where Jesus goes into His own village. Mark 6:1-6 says, *"Then He went out from there and came to His own country, and His disciples followed Him. And when the Sabbath had come, He began to teach in the synagogue. And many hearing Him were astonished, saying, 'Where did this Man get these things? And what wisdom is this which is given to Him, that such mighty works are performed by His hands! Is this not the carpenter, the Son of Mary, and brother of James, Joses, Judas, and Simon? And are not His sisters here with us?' So they were offended at Him.*

But Jesus said to them, 'A prophet is not without honor except in his own country, among his own relatives, and in his own house.' Now He could do no mighty work there, except that He laid His hands on a few sick people and healed them. And He marveled because of their unbelief. Then He went about the villages in a circuit, teaching." A few theologians think this means that their doubt was greater than His faith.

I want to suggest a thought process that I felt the Holy Spirit lead me into one day when I was struggling with this. If we look at all the verses in this passage, we see the people are very offended at Jesus. They watched Him grow up from a boy and decided that because of this, He could not be the Messiah. They were very offended at Him, and because they were offended at Him and who He was claiming to be, I think there's a good chance they would not be going to Him and asking for healing. Therefore, Jesus was not trying to pray for them, and then they weren't getting healed, because their doubt was greater than His faith. No, they would not let Him pray for them at all. They did not believe that He was the son of God, and were offended at Him.

If someone came to me and said, "I'm Santa and want to give you presents." If I didn't believe he was Santa I wouldn't want anything. Therefore, Jesus could not give the gift of healing because they did not believe he was the Messiah. They would not come to Him or let Him heal them. Just writing that out grieves my heart so much. God will always touch people if they will come to Him! When He taught people that "according to their faith they were healed," it wasn't because He couldn't do it without their faith. God created the universe with a Word of faith before any of us existed. 1 John 4:4 says, *"You are of God, little children, and have overcome them, because He who is in you is greater than He who is in the world."* If the Greater One lives inside of me, how can someone's unbelief cancel out my faith? The answer is it can't. Remember, He was only there a very short time, and suggested many times that He did not want them relying on Him physically for their healing, but on their own faith.

 If this has been a stumbling block for you, I would highly encourage you guys to look into this. Matthew 10:1 says, *"And when He had called His twelve disciples to Him, He gave them power over unclean spirits, to cast them out, and to heal all kinds of sickness and all kinds of disease."* 1 Corinthians 12:8-9 says, *"for to one is given the word of wisdom through the Spirit, to another the word of knowledge through the same Spirit, to another faith by the same Spirit, to another gifts of healings by the same Spirit."* I spent a lot of my life believing Christians had to have their own faith in order for them to get healed. My beliefs, based off of the word that the Holy Spirit has shown me and what He has backed up on the streets, is that <u>only one person needs to have true faith and expectancy.</u> It should be you, it could be them, but one person with real heart/spirit belief needs to be there! You both do not need to be in faith. Just one person, one person who has the faith of a mustard seed can move mountains. How many times did Jesus do miracles for the disciples who were in constant doubt at first? But their doubt did not cancel His faith!

This specific revelation for me has changed my life. The first time I decided to expect that everyone would get healed no matter what, I saw a guy healed who had glaucoma in his eyes; they were swollen shut. After the second or third prayer, they popped open! That same day, two other people were instantly healed. <u>Your expectancy determines your results.</u> Never let any doubt get in the way of this expectancy or it will pollute the faith that you need to get healed and heal others! Believe, believe, believe, that is the key to working in the supernatural. Even now, sometimes on my way to an outreach, I will start praying, and the Holy Spirit will show me a little doubt that has been trying to sneak in during last week. I will let it go, choose to expect, and see many healings that day.

Too Many Exceptions and Doubts

On the same note, I have heard twenty and even thirty sermons on why people don't get healed. Yet when healing, Jesus always had the same response, "because of your faith!" Let me encourage you in this; in order to heal people, you need to have your expectancy cleared of any hesitation and doubts. If you want the consistent results that you and others can count on, you need to learn how to <u>have consistent expectancy</u>, free from all doubts or reasons why they won't get healed.

Our faith needs to be pure. In Mark 11:24, Jesus says, *"if you say to this mountain and do not doubt in your heart."* To work, faith needs to be clear from doubts. I would encourage you to remove all doubts; otherwise it will be harder to get healed or be a vessel of healing. Remove any reasons for not believing. Jesus said according to your faith be it done unto you, so remove all doubt and limitations, and believe and decide to have 100% expectancy.

I remember when I was going out to pray for people one day in Downtown San Diego, I felt kind of hesitant to go. As I started to pray in the Holy Spirit, (It's so good to pray 20-30 minutes before you go, so you can set the spiritual tone for the outreach) He showed me that for the last 4 days I had a very well-hidden doubt that people would not get healed and that this doubt would get in the way of results when I was on the streets. I let go of the doubt, and started to expect that 100 percent of the people, 100 percent of the time, that day, were going to get 100 percent healed! Many times, expectancy is so key, but we will have a hidden doubt we have been believing before we go. It's normally about what's going to happen, and that prevents us from moving in the power when we start to pray for people. Take your doubts and throw them out. I like to spend some time in prayer and looking inside of myself before I go out. I first choose to be expectant from my heart and then inspect my heart for any doubts and remove them.

Add Actions to Your Faith

Faith without corresponding actions is dead. Jesus tells a story about a house built on a firm foundation in Matthew 7:24-26 and then He says this, *"Therefore whoever hears these sayings of Mine, and does them, I will liken him to a wise man who built his house on the rock: and the rain descended, the floods came, and the winds blew and beat on that house; and it did not fall, for it was founded on the rock."* I want to encourage you that it's in the doing that you'll find your faith to grow and build, adding the stability you need on your life you need. Faith is a muscle that you need to work out and to watch grow. And after a certain point, it feels like riding a bicycle. I know that everyone I pray for will get healed. And I know that God will show up.

Jesus is saying that your life will not be firmly established until you start "doing the gospel." You will not be on a firm foundation until you start going, you will not be completely solidified until you start moving. You will not be completely safe or on an established foundation until you start acting on the Word of God. In other words, as you hit the streets and stores and start to heal others, you will find your greatest faith for your own and your family's needs.

My good friend Art Montgomery had to stand against cancer when it attacked his wife and when it was in every cell of her body, but seeing Jesus heal many people on the streets over time, helped him so much. By the end of it, his wife who had cancer in every cell of her body was completely, completely healed in Jesus name and you can be too :) !

Do Miracles Operate by Gift or Faith?

This is one of my favorite questions. It goes back to 1 Corinthians 12:8-9, *"...for to one is given the word of wisdom through the Spirit, to another the word of knowledge through the same Spirit, to another faith by the same Spirit, to another gifts of healings by the same Spirit..."* People take this verse as an excuse for not moving in the power of God or not going on the streets and reaching out to hurting people with God's power; "it's not my gift" they say. This section should help a lot with bringing understanding to this.

In Mark 16:17 Jesus says *"And these signs will follow those who believe: In My name they will cast out demons; they will speak with new tongues;"* "these signs will follow <u>those who believe</u>" (not those who are gifted) and He lists healing, deliverance, etc. Then if we look further in the gospels, we see the disciples asking Jesus why they can't do some of the miracles He does. He always says it's because they need to have faith, not that they need a gift of healing or whatever. Even when He says because of prayer and fasting, He says first, because of your unbelief!

Does Mark 16:17 disagree with 1 Corinthians 12:8-9? No definitely not, they were both written through men by the same Holy Spirit and He is not confused. We can and should, according to Jesus's great commission, operate in every sign of God's power without a gift in it. We just have to use our faith and practice to develop it over time. This is different than having a gift in one of these areas.

Think about it this way, all of us can run and all of us, if we practice, can run well; but a gifted runner doesn't need to practice to maintain their gift. The word gift in the Greek is "charisma" and one of the better defining qualities of this word is a "spiritual grace." Remember that a grace is something that is a not earned, but is a free gift. A gift is just a fully or mostly developed version of the same thing every Christian needs to activate in our personal ministries through our faith and practice.

Even if someone were to disagree with that, which I think is biblically very difficult, in 1 Corinthians 14:1, Paul teaches us to *"pursue love, and desire spiritual gifts, but especially that you may prophesy."* The solution to not having a gift is to *"But earnestly desire the best gifts..."* (1 Corinthians 12:31) So let's ask and desire all the best gifts, and if we have an absence of a gifting in an area, let's use our faith and practice to get the job done anyway! Never let an absence of a gifting give you an excuse to bury your talents or stop you from fulfilling the great commission through God's power. Remember that every Christian has a *"measure of faith"* (Romans 12:3). According to Jesus, faith is a gift that is big enough to move in any supernatural act that is needed to fulfill Mark 16 and the great commission in the absence of a fully developed gift.

I might also make the argument that initially, it's better to not have a gift in something, because then you have to practice it on your own and grow your faith. Jesus said in John 20:29 *"Blessed are they that have not seen and yet have believed"*.

B. Research, Activation, and Resources
Reading

    Bible - At least three chapters a day, beginning in Matthew.

Speaking

    Commit to saying again and believing ten times a day: "100% of the time, 100% of the people, get 100% healed the first time!"

Doing

    Complete all Activation homework!

1. Decide to keep your faith free from exceptions, doubts and any theology that would fill it with unbelief instead of expectancy.

2. Take some time and remove any doubts you may have.

3. Is there any reason I think people won't get healed when I pray for them? I am not worthy, I have not been doing it long enough? I am not anointed enough? According to Jesus removing doubts from your HEART is very important.

Passing

☐ Have you practiced turning your brain off?

☐ Have you had the opportunity to and chosen to not rationalize why people don't get healed, but to simply believe? Please explain.

_____

_____

_____

_____

_____

_____

_____

☐ Have you read the next Week in your workbook?

☐ Have you watched "Tips & Demo on Healing & How Not to Lose It?"

☐ Have you watched "How to Get Boldness in 5 Minutes to Demonstrate Miracles?"

☐ Have you chosen to set aside time this week for quiet time and reading and praying? Please expound.

_____

_____

_____

_____

_____

_____

_____

Conclusion

We believe 100% that this workbook has empowered you to walk in and become the man and women that you were called into becoming! Our goal has been to:

- ☐ train you with teaching and hands-on-training in how to become a man or woman who operates in the full Mark 16 gospel.
- ☐ train up soldiers, but skilled warriors and skilled harvesters who will take back the kingdom of heaven from darkness and from a spirit of religion and apathy that has settled on Christianity in America.
- ☐ walk in enough power and demonstration of the Holy Spirit and love
- ☐ take back America for the King of Kings and the LION OF JUDAH

We will leave you with this...

Mark 16: *"Go into all the world and preach the gospel to every creature. He who believes and is baptized will be saved, but he who does not believe will be condemned.*

And these signs will follow those who believe!

    1. In My name, they will cast out demons.

    2. They will speak with new tongues.

    3. They will take up serpents.

    4. And if they drink anything deadly, it will by no means hurt them.

    5. They will lay hands on the sick, and they will recover."

Guys and gals GO and bring the gospel to everyone. Do it by miracles and preaching. When people get saved, disciple them in the same things. Let's turn this country upside down with the gospel and the FIRE of heaven!

So much love on each of you sons, daughters and warriors for Jesus Christ and the Kingdom of Heaven!

75733185R00065

Made in the USA
Columbia, SC
25 September 2019